Who is the Black Queen Calafía of Golden California?

The Real WonderWoman
3rd edition

By MS. TAMRA L. DICUS

Published by CALIFORNIA IS ME™.

CALIFORNIA IS ME ™ is an imprint under CALIFORNIA IS ME, LLC.

Library of Congress Control Number: 2018903283

ISBN-13: **978-0-9742010-1-6**

ISBN-10: 0974201014

DEDICATION

For the silent souls who cry out but are never heard.
For those who say, "the truth gets buried and
is never told."
Know that what goes on in the dark, comes to light.
Know what you teach can be taught.
Know what you learn can be unlearned.[1]

Special dedication is extended toward my niece and nephews and future children. I hope they will one day be judged off character only and can see this dream realized.

I love you, Keir, Kai and Judah!

"But still, I rise." Thank you, My Show-Me-Stater Ms. Maya Angelou

Infinite thanks to my ancestors.

---

1 The movie Star Wars character Jedi Master Yoda said, "You must unlearn what you have learned."

CONTENTS

FOREWORD

"The long lost Queen has risen again to take her rightful place on her throne as the regal, shinning embodiment of elegance, beauty, courage and wisdom. In these pages, Queen Calafia comes to life to remind us to claim our sovereignty, our heritage and our sacred birthright inheritance to dignity and human respect. A consummate historian and advocate, Dicus does a marvelous job bringing this lost treasure to new generations of young readers with historical integrity and sensibility. Today, we are all Queen Calafia."

- Professor Maurice Dyson, Professor of Law at Thomas Jefferson School of Law, San Diego, California

ABOUT THIS BOOK

This book requires that we must go backwards in order to go forward. Yuck, I know, history, right? First of all, do not let anyone tell you that history is boring. I had to learn that. In the words of author, orator, political theorist and philosopher, Edmund Burke, "Those who don't know history are doomed to repeat it." Thus, if we don't love or even like our own history, we *will* be history. We are going to sail the seas where history will guide us to the discovery of the golden path of truth. Don't let these words shock you! Education of any kind is necessary to help you succeed in life. In fact, the California Constitution declares education is a right. [2]

I discovered this golden truth last summer in Washington, D.C. on the way to California bound for law school. While the movie, Wonder Woman soared to historic blockbuster heights, I felt as invisible as the glass plane Wonder Woman piloted. I hope by reading this book you will see the importance of history and education. The 'golden sword of truth' held by the Nubian Queen Calafía, along with history, science, math, logic and a little common sense are about all you'll need to unearth one of California's deepest and, yes, 'darkest secrets'. Ok, so, let's get started by setting the scene. Imagine you are invited to a friend's house party. As you approach, you hear music blaring from outside the door.

---

2 Under the California Constitution, public education is "uniquely a fundamental concern of the State and prohibits maintenance and operation of the common public school system in a way which denies basic educational equality to the students. The State itself bears the ultimate authority and responsibility to ensure that its district-based system of common schools provides basic equality of educational opportunity." Butt v. California, 4 Cal. 4th 668, 685 (1992).

You open the door, step inside, and after making a grand entrance, not even your friend who invited you introduces you at the party. They ignore you. How do you feel? Your friend is called "History". Let's go backwards a bit into time. Buckle up and hold on!

We are now in the 16th Century when "Queen Calafía", the legendary ruler of "California", first appeared. Are you still with me? In his Spanish romance novel, Las Sergas de Esplandián written in 1510, Garcí Rodríguez (or Ordoñez) de Montalvo depicted her the proud ruler of California and as the wondrous, fierce leader of an island inhabited by Black warrior women who lived in the fashion of Amazons, on an island of solid gold.

Allow me to reintroduce the black Queen Calafía, in my own fun little way. I hope to shed light on this magnificent find, a gold nugget of truth. I am the spiritual descent of Queen Calafía who reigns from Kansas City, Missouri, the monarchial and royal place of the originator of the mastermind of imagination. So, naturally my parents thought the family should travel to California, twice, to visit its famous magical amusement park.

Had we only known in the 20th century that a 16th century story like this existed and its significance in history, we would have a spark of hope to have been encouraged in so many ways. America's first chocolate superheroes were named California!

So, like Toni Morrison instructed, I have chosen to write what I wish I would have had in my youth. So step inside my mind, grab a young person or adult and participate in the fun discoveries ahead! (See Morrison's quote: "If there's a book you want to read, but it hasn't been written yet, then you must write it." Here: https://twitter.com/tonimorrrison/status/395708227888771072).

Well, maybe you've wondered about "why" this book's title has the state name of California (if you know California is a state by now or not) tied to her mythical ruler, Queen Calafía. Let this story inspire ladies to become confident in our identity as black females in the Americas. Let gentlemen celebrate women also in all that we are and birth into this world. Maybe like me, your image was teased growing up; or you were told of man's inhumanity to mankind.

So, grab a person by the hand and tell her or him this story. We can all be a hero or *she-ro* and participate in storytelling for education. The best way to learn something yourself is to teach others. Booker T. Washington yearned for ones to, "...lift themselves up in proportion as they help to lift others..." in his book, Up from Slavery. Benjamin Franklin said, "Tell me and I forget. Teach me and I remember. Involve me and I learn." Martin Luther King, Jr. said, "The function of education is to teach one to think intensively and to think critically. Intelligence plus character - that is the goal of true education."

PREFACE

Are you stuck in a "why" phase? Does your mind constantly spin wondering why and then asking another why even after an initial explanation is given? Maybe why there is a universe? Why you aren't accepted? Why someone is not friendly to you? You must use your imagination and innate logic to piece together clues to answer the proverbial $64,000 question: why. Don't worry, I know you are smart and are ready for the challenge! Curiosity helps solve problems. Curiosity produces creation. Curiosity helps breed imagination. Imagination is powerful as it spurs innovation and yields solutions to vexing problems. Imagination gives way to discovery. Discovery gives way to inventions. Inventions drive technology. Technology makes improvements to make our lives better. Imagery is powerful because it directly relates to how we treat others. Names are unique because they are the fastest way to identify the images we see.

The 21st Century has already been characterized by innovative leaps in technology that have solved problems that were once deemed unsolvable. In the 14th century, intractable problems were solved because of the quest for knowledge. Before there were maps, before there were compasses, before there were computers (the human and machine types), there was only the land, the stars, the sea, and the human brain. Time is important because it serves as a reference point for the past, present, and future. Before the United States ever came into existence, there were lands and "territories". Explorers from Europe began to travel and migrate to this "New World", named "America" for Italian explorer, Amerigo Vesspuci, in the late 1400s. During this time, there were no correct maps of the world. There were no real communication tools, like cellular (cell) phones or telephones commonly used today. Can you imagine yourself traveling without directions or communications equipment ensure your safe return home? Scary! Well, with no maps, compasses, or tasty food, wouldn't you want to know how to obtain what you don't know and don't have? Enter travel. Spices such as cinnamon was in high demand and worth more than precious currency!

The quest for spices is a similar journey we must take to find the black Queen Calafía. This story is the evolution of the black Queen Calafía and her majestic California dynasty of black women warrior Amazons. It is a quest to discover how she originally came to be magically transformed from fantasy to reality. To solve this quest, requires imagination and creativity. So, pay close attention as disclosed herein is an Ancient Spanish and American Civil War hidden gem...

1 GOLDEN GROUNDS

Hello, how are you?

In Spanish that's: *Hola, ¿cómo estás?*

I am the golden sword of truth.

It's very nice to meet you!

Yes, I talk, so I can protect you.

It is said that, "The pen is mightier than the sword."

Well, I'd like to think that I am a good representation of what it means to slay with my words and so I'll function as both!"

Who is Queen Calafía (In Spanish it is *?Quienes es Reina Calafía?*), the black queen who is the ruler of the golden warrior island, called *California*?

A mysterious name it sounds.

And speaking on sounds, if you don't know how to pronounce a word, that's what friends are for! Just ask a friend who speaks the language you seek to speak.

Have you heard of a black woman warrior Amazon queen named "Calafía" who reigned over the strongest land in the world?

No?

Have you seen Her Majesty, the black, powerful Queen Calafía on her golden island where only black women lived called "California" (In Spanish black women is *mujeres negras*)?

No?

Well, I hadn't either, until I met her. But then a wicked storm washed her away and we had to separate. So, can you help me find the mysterious, majestic black queen of California, Queen Calafía (In Spanish her name is *Reina Calafía*)? For I lost my dear friend but will fill you in on what I can recall anyway. I will navigate the story and tell you a bit of her character at the same time. Put on your logic caps for this quest to find her, you will surely need it. I must throw in a little exercise to make sure you're up for the challenge. I will be a truthful guide and faithful friend.

Well, in the days of explorers, sailboats were used to gain knowledge of new places they had never been. Just like NASA does today, astronauts use spaceships to explore outer space.

NASA's California gem, a black woman, Katherine Johnson, mathematically catapulted America's first man into our black universe in 1961!

So, as we travel this journey and sail the seas,

To make sure we find her, we need to fix and

focus our eyes to see

The legendary, mysterious, majestic black Queen Calafía,

On her magical, golden California island that she resides.

It is said that she is the most powerful of them all

Because her golden isle *is* the strongest, and most courageous in the entire world.

Because the mighty California women warriors had superior strength of ten thousand men, passionate courage like a lioness, and beautiful bodies that were large and muscular where the warmth of the sun kissed their skin. They were simply a complete wonder as they comprised all of the best traits wrapped in one body.

Rewind the time and image where you had only seen little birds, and then all of a sudden, your eyes see dinosaurs! When at first you fix your eyes upon such an amazing creature, you are most certainly caught in a wondrous daze, capturing all the features.

So all were amazed at Queen Calafía in particular because she also had extraordinary strength,

That all were in shock that any woman could achieve as much as she did, so effortlessly and most of the time, single handedly.

Her Majesty's Californians shocked and stunned several men, by their mere presence, they kept pulling them in and at the same time, made some of them want to duck, hide, and run away from them for the power was too much!

You see, many are mesmerized by the natural brilliance of gold and diamonds, they either desire and want them or become envious, jealous, and must take them.

While others get blinded by the brilliance of shiny things and turn their heads away as it is too much for their eyes to see. However, know that no matter how one feels,

Nothing can stop the diamond from sparkle.

Nothing can stop the gold from shine.

For it is just inherent in the nature of them to exude beauty from within.

All the more reason, this is why many came to seek out their island, even little boys and girls, as all wondered just how in the world they came to be, as they were truly *extra*ordinary.

At any rate, all of the island and the world began to take note. "California, the wondrous, warrior women!" they'd exclaim. "California, the wonderous, warrior women!" they'd repeat. Some liked this chant and others did not.

So as you can see, because of jealousy, it is important to ensure that we find the real Queen Calafía

As we want to avoid the dangers of lies.

I, the Golden Sword, can help cut through the dangers that may arise.

Lies can lead us down a wrong, long and winding path

And we don't ever want to go down that!

You see when we hide the truth

It hurts our brains and causes pain.

The truth doesn't take much effort so it's easy to avoid the rain.

You may walk solidly and securely down the straight path of right.

As honesty is the best policy and is guided by my golden light.

So, let's illuminate the truth and forever shine it bright!

Let's continue to read to discover and sail this journey together

In the powerful Pacific seas of the wavy, endless ocean blue.

In the end to prove our collection of clues that we find

on our path to ultimately, magically come true!

We can use our ears to hear and our eyes to see

So, let's together solve this hidden puzzle of a mystery!

2 GOLDEN GEMS

Next, I'll ask Mister Mango and his cousin, Mister Orange too!

They saw her and said she has a full, round figure like theirs. The roundness of a woman's figure is to increase the population,

As she is the world's mother of all creation!

Now it's time for a fun science break! There are mysteries in the makings of combining things.

Science says the first origin of man is found in African lands. Biology gives us a clue in that the Negroid gene is the dominate gene while the Caucasoid gene is the recessive gene. Genes are called "DNA" it is the makeup of what makes you, you. DNA makes human beings individually unique. They are also called “traits”.

That’s why a majority of the earth’s peoples have a powerful, protective pigment called “melanin” as it is a natural sun ray protectant (but as times have progressed, sunscreen we should still seek). As people traveled, some didn’t need to have such a high amount of it in their skin.

Also genes show up in a majority of earth’s people traits that have straight hair and brown eyes. While a minority of people’s genes have cool, colored blue-green eye genes and have luscious curly hair genes that is soft like wool. So the combination of luscious curls and highly concentrated melanin in skin, is surely one of the most unique walking human beings!

Thus, Africa’s black woman is the first woman on Earth and the birth giver to all. Ancient Egyptians deemed the color “black” is closet to God and they were full of melanin, thus this is a good name. So, you see, we are all unique people of the human race. So, thanks to the black woman, we can stretch up and grow up tall!

Given set of facts: Google or imagine or draw a pear and a cucumber.

Question: Which is the round shape?

Act: Slay the straight shape. Circle the round shape.

We are all diverse and designed with a purpose.

Remember, it matters not the exterior, what matters is the interior- what do you want to contribute with your one life?

The word “queen” also means she’s definitely a woman, since a queen wears a crown.

Just like your mama who makes cookies in the oven, she sure can lay it down!

Like a woman who balances and runs her house,

Is the black Queen Calafía who rules her isle,

The California island is also known as a "Terrestrial Paradise" for it is the Garden of Eden of all creation.

A "golden island" means it's a piece of land on the Earth with solid gold pockets in the ground and sprinkled golden minerals in the sand,

Surrounded by the bluest of waters against the curvy coasted land against wavy oceans and powerful seas. We are on our way indeed to solving this mystery.

"Amazon" means women that are courageous, both physically and mentally strong.

Can you hug a strong mother, strong sister, or a strong woman?

Know a powerful woman is a queen and she wears a precious crown to show she is different and commands to be respected. On California, all of the black warrior

Californians agreed to make the beautiful, powerful and smart black Calafía the queen leader.

All were excited to join in her army and everyone went to meet and greet her.

You see the Queen Calafía was the one and only who had the most beauty and extraordinary strength, wrapped in courage to solve the most difficult of problems.

She battled knights with the strength of a man, and her sister, Liota, helped from time to time and was Calafía's bodyguard. So all could not simply resist calling her *the* wonder queen woman. As she is so fierce, so fearless and so smart (like you, she loves to read too!).

She's also so courageous to boot.

No one in the world can touch her as she outsmarts them all. She is the most valued having many attributes; no one can replace her, short or tall.

Given set of facts: Google or imagine or draw a hat and a crown.

Question: Which one is a crown?

Act: Slay the hat, circle the crown.

Can you place a sparkly tiara on your head or a female's head?

3 GOLDEN SWORD

Oh, and when she travels, don't forget, she has me,

The protective golden sword of truth, resting on her hip,

To avoid future misery

When she travels the sea miles as she steers her ship

Just in case she needs to protect herself from stranger dangers on a trip.

Why one time, I, the Golden Sword of Truth, recall saying, "My Queen, hold up, wait. Do you know what I see? A storm is developing. I see some pirates coming out from the sea trying to steal our gold booty! Word travels fast and I know they now see our carpeted coast of pearls with gold peaking from under the sand. Hurry up, run fast! Queen Calafía you must tell your warrior girls!"

Queen Calafía replied, "Scoff! There is no need to run, but I will solidly walk and handle this pesky little threat. Tisk, tisk! What a shame, someone's always trying to take something that's not theirs. Let's go get 'em girls!"

Queen Calafía sprang into action, straightened her back in a solid stance and commanded her voice to cry out her demands.

She cried out, "Stay away strangers, for I will protect my girls! We are California warriors, the wondrous ones; I know you've heard of us! We sail the seas with power and might. We fight for our rights! I will ensure that you remember my name! Say it out loud! Come near me if you dare, but I am Queen Calafía, the strongest wondrous warrior out here!" Her voice echoed and bounced from all the rocky pearlescent shores, golden mountains and luscious lands. That is what the black Queen Calafía commanded.

A queen sits on not just a chair, but on a golden throne

She makes good choices for all those she considers her own.

Protecting her army with the aid of griffins and

helping her monarchy gain wisdom

As she is the only one who has the keen vision.

Given set of facts: Draw a chair and a throne (you may use Google or imagine one).

Question: Where is the throne?

Act: Slay the chair, circle the throne.

Can you sit on or find a fancy golden chair or ask a female sit on a fancy golden chair? You may paint it or image it. Just draw it if you must. Envision yourself on the throne and what that must feel like.

A queen rocks the *flyest* jewelry

Richly adorned with African yellow gold, African blue, white, and black sparkly diamonds, and

African emerald green precious stones.

Draped around her neck are American oval white pearls

She is a wealthy lady and must show the world

So all can know that she is a very special girl

Given: In chemistry, the Periodic Chart of Elements states "Au" is gold and "Ag" is silver. ("Au" is easier to remember over silver - the jingle to memorize is: "Hey, you stole my gold!")

Write the elements on a piece of paper.

Question: Which is gold?

Act: Slay the silver. Circle the gold.

Can you place a golden ring on your finger or the finger of a female?

Can you place a golden bracelet on your wrist or the wrist of a female?

Can you pace a string of pearls around your neck or the neck of a female?

If you don't have the jewelry, that's ok,

For Her Majesty the black Queen Calafía would command

"You must make do with what you got!"

"Why, you can make jewelry out of sparkly mineral rocks! Simply take a gold marker and color them!"

So now that we have collected a few more clues.

She had to live close to someone right?

4 GOLDEN FRIENDS

So, let's ask again my friend Miss Midnight Blue

She can whisper to the wind, to direct us to answer where she lives.

Miss Midnight Blue says, "Last time I saw her, The Queen Calafía lived next to a neighbor with some height." The wind was familiar too, with the beautiful, wonderful, wild, and wavy green leaves of my friend, Miss Palm Tree.

Miss Palm Tree's luscious leaves waved "Hi!" as they swayed back and forth in the dark midnight sky.

Miss Palm Tree says, "Because I saw Queen Calafía with the same pattern of wonderful, wild and wavy hair that I noticed her bouncy, curly curls too. And she had such versatility that she wore her locks of hair in several cool different ways, in braids or corn rows or straight or just let it go as an afro."

Miss Palm Tree also says, "The hair of the Queen Calafía is like wool, soft yet strong, And it's like the branches of my palm tree, so this kind of hair lasts the years long! If God grants you blessings to age old, then you'll need strong hair that will grow with you year to year. "

Given set of facts: Google or imagine or draw a Palm Tree and an Oak Tree .
Question: Which image is a palm tree?
Act: Slay the oak tree branch, circle the palm tree.

A queen's presence commands power as her passionate voice does too

All rise as soon as she walks in the room

She flaunts her fashionable golden skirt so

All eyes stare watching and awaiting her every move.

Given set of facts: Google or imagine or draw pants or a skirt.

Question: Can you pick between the pants and skirt?

Act: Slay the pants, Circle the skirt.

Can you tie a golden tutu around your waist or a female's waist? Or maybe a gold piece of fabric? Or just envision it if you must.

Remember, Queen Calafía commands that you must always, "Make do with what you got, Darling!"

She also wears a 100% pure golden armor vest

to protect her heart

For she is mega, mighty, and brilliantly smart.

Given: Job A: A person picks up sparkly starpowder from the Moon earned $50. Job B: an engineer solves how stars travel in outer space near Mars earned $100.

Question: Would you be an engineer who solves problems or a person who picks starpowder?

Act: Your choice here, there is truly no right answer. The benefits of picking starpowder is that you can touch and eye the sparkle starpowder powers that transfers to you! The benefits of solving how stars travel is to learn how to move and become as brilliant as the stars! So, slay or pick either within the zone of your natural abilities. As long as you achieve your full potential, joy is in all types work. Whatever you choose, there is value in finding your passion, as it helps avoid the blues.

Can you wrap an invisible, protective sword around you? It will guard you!

Can you put your arms through a gold vest or a female's arms?

So maybe Her Majesty has her arms to lift her trustworthy golden sword and if we ask a friend, maybe he can clue us in?

We have a couple of clues to help us avoid the blues.

Oh, and it's ok to ask for help. I'll ask my friends for clues,

I'll introduce you to Miss Midnight Blue

She knows what she looks like because she's black like her too.

As the darkness of the night

Is the only way to see the stars that shine bright!

Miss Midnight blue spoke of her attitude too:

"She is kind but not a push-over,

So she has a passionate, loving heart

But she struggles how to balance it with her smarts.

She regulates but doesn't retaliate,

Unless one strikes her first.

So, she is fair and just and only slays if she must.

She is also regal, so she has a Code of Conduct."

Our friend, Chief Stone Mountain speaks.

He says, "I taught her how to have faith as big as me. For this is the way she can help protect her amazing Amazon army from harm. I taught her to help her use her faith in herself and in God, to make her arms strong like me and unbreakable, you see. So, wherever she is, I know she's using them."

Her mission is in life is to keep all safe from violence

To protect all from strange intruders coming ashore on the island.

Declare or ask a female to announce and say out loud:

"I am a lady, respect I command!

I will protect myself, my family and my friends!"

Let's also ask the pearly white Señora Seashell

To find out more to open the wisdom door.

She says you should open her mirror shell

To help release the magical spell.

Wait! Look!

Run quickly to a mirror. Do you see her in the mirror?

It is your reflection and at last we found her! Eureka!

YOU are the real vision of Queen Calafía

YOU are the wondrous, beauty warrior that you seek,

Soooo super smart, courageous, beautiful, and strong.

Queen Calafía says, "I rest and reside deep within you! So, make me proud and make your daily presence known!"

So, I am glad you solved the puzzle and found yourself in me,

For we share the same identity.

Know like California warriors, you too are not only a wonder, but an unbreakable warrior.

You must have the passion of an engineer to solve problems and the passion of care,

Like the Queen Calafía California black women Amazon Warriors, to provide solutions if you so dare!

It's Sharing Time! Let me share with you a bit on the name transformation from Queen Calafía herself!

3 GOLDEN MYSTERY

QUEEN CALAFÍA SPEAKS

"Hello, queens and kings! I am Queen Calafía, the Queen of California, and my island is named after me, Calafía. Maybe you've heard of the word "California" as a state? I am the namesake of the state and no worries and no shade toward my justice friend, Wonder Woman, she can be the wonder, while my California Amazons will forever be the warriors! Consequently, my warrior island name is the oldest state name in the history of the United States! I breathed life from my California island and exhaled the real state name since a Spanish man, a *conquistador* named Hernan Cortés, was inspired by me and actually believed my large, Amazonian ladies existed in reality from reading the mythical, majestic, thrilling romance novel. Through war and pain, I searched for love and married King Talanque, California's first king!"

Queen Calafia Courtesy of CALIFORNIA IS ME illustration credit, Daniel Bamber

My name, Calafía, is the core meaning and root of the word, "California" as the first syllables sound the same when saying the root word "*khalifa*" in Arabic or "caliph" or "califa" in English. It means a male leader. The Spanish use the "a" to denote a female, so my name is a unique Arabic-Spanish name meaning a female leader or a queen warrior! I yearn to one day see my now state will adopt me and my warrior Amazons as official like shown on the right below. The current seal is on the left. Would you like to help me?"

State of California
Cal Gov Code § 400 Link here: https://codes.findlaw.com/ca/government-code/gov-sect-400.html
(see pg. 86 for color link)

The Missing Great Seal,

Courtesy of CALIFORNIA IS ME, illustration credit, LaMont Russ

Well, isn't that something, the State of California is named after you too! Your image as a woman, your likeness as the choice human being for the state name. What major importance to our heritage! Women, were often used as inspiration to uncover the then, unknown shape of the world with the help of the Astrolabe and compass. Such navigational tools were developed by countries of Andalusia (or al-Andalus now Spain [so named in Alabama and Pennsylvania]), China and Greece. Also there are cities named after California in Missouri and Maryland). Once the Spanish explorers read about me and my mystical land on the journey to what was a "new world", they marveled at the beautiful real curvaceous terrain and coast with golden shores and pearls. A light bulb went off as they surveyed the land to name such a beautiful land, "C. California" in honor of me and my ladies. See page 69. The actual State of California is wrapped in your name, too— strong, courageous, and beautiful black warriors! So, have no fear, solve problems, rise and reign!"

History and Science Break

In Las Sergas de Esplandían, Queen Calafía is a Moor as are her monarchy of California. According to ancient history, the Moors are descendants of Berbers, like Egyptians, are indigenous of Africa. Such names mean "black" (i.e. higher concentrations of melanin pigment from black to brown in skin comparative to those with the least amount of melanin) skin color and hair of wool. High concentrations of melanin are also found in the skin of *Negroid* or Negro or *negras* (in Spanish) people. Thus, the two authors, Mr. Rodríguez de Montalvo and Mr. Hale, communicated this important ethnic "color" distinction (today's African Americans, Afro-Latinos, mixed, "biracial").

Queen Calafía Courtesy of CALIFORNIA IS ME illustration credit, Daniel Bamber

"I am Queen Calafía, I will forever reign California!"

"The Amazon river in South America is named after us too!"

5 GOLDEN HISTORY

The etymology (fancy name for the origins of a word) of the name "California" was discovered by Rev. Mr. Edward Everett Hale.

ACT: compare and contrast the given information below.

Given A:

shall hear." In the midst of this great crusade, every word of which, of course, is the most fictitious of fiction, appear the episodes which describe California and its Queen.

First, of California itself here is the description: —

"Now you are to hear the most extraordinary thing that ever was heard of in any chronicles or in the memory of man, by which the city would have been lost on the next day, but that where the danger came, there the safety came also. Know, then, that, on the right hand of the Indies, there is an island called California, very close to the side of the Terrestrial Paradise,* and it was peopled by black women, without any man among them, for they lived in the fashion of Amazons. They were of strong and hardy bodies, of ardent courage and great force. Their island was the strongest in all the world, with its steep cliffs and rocky shores. Their arms were all of gold, and so was the harness of the wild beasts which they tamed and rode. For, in the whole island, there was no metal but gold. They lived in caves wrought

She was not *petite*, nor blond, nor golden-haired. She was large and black as the ace of clubs. But the prejudice of color did not then exist even among the most brazen-faced or the most copper-headed. For, as you shall learn, she was reputed the most beautiful of women; and it was she, O Californians, who wedded the gallant prince Talanque, — your first-known king. The supporters of the arms of the beautiful shield of the State of California should be, on the right,

Given A source: Rev. Mr. Edward Everett Hale, The Queen of California, The Atlantic Monthly, March 1864, at Page 266. Courtesy of the Library of Congress, Washington, D.C. microfilm

Given B: "[W]hen two of the knights, Talanque and Maneli, saw what <u>wonders the Queen</u> was doing they attacked her with the greatest fury, as if they considered her absolutely insane." – emphasis intentional.

Given B source: Translated "Las Sergas de Esplandaian" by George Davidson, "The Origin and the Meaning of the Name California : Calafia the Queen of the Island of California," published by San Francisco : Geographical Society of the Pacific, 1910, at page 41

Question: Prior to the time of the creation of Wonder Woman circa 1940, what were the obvious blends of written information above (in Given A and B) available to inspire/create a "wonder woman"?

By substituting "woman" for "queen" with the story of A, it would have been obvious circa 1940 to invent Wonder Woman from Queen Calafía. So, since California is in your heart now, maybe you'd like to visit the state one day and discover more magical places. To be the queen that helps to solve more mysteries. In all nooks and crannies and spaces. Queen Calafía commands you to:

Imagine. Solve. Act.

Dream. Think. Create.

CULTURAL COMPARISONS

QUEEN CALAFIA (circa 1510) VERSUS WONDER WOMAN® (circa 1940) KEYS

QUEEN CALAFIA AND black women	WONDER WOMAN®
1. Terrestrial Paradise Island (aka Garden of Eden)	Paradise Island
2. Ruler of island of California	Island has been off coast of Pacific Ocean of California
3. Golden island of golden *armas* or weapons, sword, and shield	Golden Armor, sword, shield and ironic golden lasso of truth
4. Island is described as near Asia or Right hand of Indies	Globe of Asia in comics shown in DC Comics #1
5. Queen is a wonder to men	Name is wonder woman with a crown
6. Real chains on black women and Slavery	Chains of prejudice and male superiority
7. Traits: not petite , powerful, black hair (Serena Williams)	Traits: not petite, powerful, hair is not blond
8. California black Amazon warriors rode wild beasts	Wonder Woman road a wild horse

With these precious facts, esteem yourself; lift yourself; develop yourself! In fact, William Moulton Marston thought the new women, because they have caring hearts, would be "rulers of the world".* If you are curious now and want more information on the Queen Calafía of California and wonder what has been done further to help Queen Calafía be restored to her throne in the Great Seal, stay tuned for the next stage. Stay tuned for my next book. To celebrate Queen Calafía's throne and feel empowered knowing the original, real, and first American superhero was the Queen Calafía's California warriors, check out: www.caliisme.com/products for the empowering

CALFORNIA IS ME® fashion product line.

WARNING: Upon wearing the CALIFORNIA IS ME® gear, you will become enlightened, powerful, and intelligent to take up the sword of the pen.

*Upon examining the Papers of William Moulton Marston, 1896-1947, MC 920, at Schlesinger Library, Harvard University, an interview recorded on a paper titled, "The Amazon". The paper discloses a letter dated April 16, 1942 that Marston wrote to Sheldon Mayer on the Amazon history of the "Amazon-Aphrodite-Athena method" creating daughters living on a Paradise Island for the concept of *Wonder Woman*; however, nothing to the "exact process" as it "remains cloaked in mystery". See another clue at pg. 64. Special thanks to two ladies at Harvard University: 1) The Curator for Race and Ethnicity at Schlesinger Library, Radcliffe Institute for Advanced Study, Harvard University, Dr. Kenvi Phillips guided me and informed me that Mercedes, from the unabridged version of Alexander Dumas' (of African descent) classic novel and my favorite movie, The Count of Monte Cristo, is a black woman; and 2) Jennifer Fauxsmith for helping me with the search!

Learn to fight with knowledge and arm yourselves with its power of reading and writing! You must learn to appreciate and develop keen wisdom and knowledge that is as sharp as the golden sword of truth, for it will protect you! The truth shall set you free! You are royalty.

For more info on NASA's Katherine Johnson, Mary Jackson, and Dorothy Vaughan, see here:

https://www.nasa.gov/modernfigures/education-resources

For more info on how I and others became an engineer, see here: http://www.nacme.org/engineered-stories-for-you and read the article on Thomas Fuller, the prodigy African calculator shipped to Alexandria, Virginia as a slave in 1724 to show blacks are not mentally inferior to whites (see link in bibliography). Tons of golden information to help start a career in engineering are at: http://www.nacme.org and http://www.nsbe.org. For more resources, video, links, see http://www.caliisme.com/secrets (enter code: QueenCalafia)

EXTENSIVE THANKS

God and Christ, my family, inclusive of my Aunt Ruth, Grandma Betty and Grandpa Pete (R.I.P.), my parents, uncles, brothers, niece, nephews, and cousins from California, Florida, Kansas, Maryland, Missouri, Pennsylvania, and Texas. My friends Ahmed, Aristotle, Anastasia, Annette, Amelia, Briana, Bridget, Brandon, Bruce, Camie, Carissa, Chuck, Cleo, Danelle, Daniel, Dagmar, Damien, Darah, Darius, Dee, Drew, Eric, Ervina, Gordon, Greg, Hannah, Ivy, Jamila, Jaracus, Jennifer, Jess, Joel, Jonathan, Kenneth, Lamont, Lei-Chala, Lesli, Lisa, Laura, Maiesha, Marcy, Marshon, Mindy, Michael, Monica G., Monica S., Nakia, Niki, Octavia, Pam, Paul, Rashida, Rome, Ryan, Sarah, Sharon, Scott, Tameka, Tashiana, Tiaka, Tshung-Yin, and all others who have helped in conversation to achieve this dream. All librarians at the Library of Congress and archivists at the U.S. National Archives Museum, Washington D.C.:

Sara, Sybil, Mr. Bell, J.; PTO friends and all at the Alexander in Virginia, St. James-Paseo United Methodist Church in Missouri, Ebenezer A.M.E. and Reid Temple church members, Maryland, NSBE, D.C., Friendship Collegiate Academy Public Charter School, D.C., law and engineering students and friends at University of California, San Diego, the Fab4, Dean Bullock and Professors Bisom-Rapp, Dyson, Greene, Rierson, Semeraro, Vandeveld and Wildenthal at Thomas Jefferson School of Law, Professor Fluker and alumni family at Tuskegee University. Thanks to friends from Africa's Egypt, Lybia, and Nigeria, China, Germany, Mexico, Spain, Turkey, and the U.S.A. Eternal thanks to the Information Age, Google™, the State of California, and the Antiquarian Society of Boston for introducing me to Reverend Dr. Edward Everett Hale, the mastermind Garcí Rodríguez (or Ordóñez) de Montalvo, and my kindred spirit, Niki de Saint Phalle, despite uninterest, sculpted the truth in *Queen Califia's Magical Circle* park in *Escondido, California. Thank you, Leah Goodwin. Thank you, William Thomas Little for staying faithful to the Spanish[3], Professors Alkebulan and Ambers, the Kansas City Call and AFRO newspapers. ASALH, and the African American Civil War Memorial Museum, D.C. Visit also the African Latin museum, Casa del Rey Moro, in San Diego, CA. Disclaimer: The views expressed herein are my own as a private citizen and not of the U.S. Federal Government or the USPTO.

*Escondido is Spanish for "hidden valley" in English. How mystical right? We are no longer hidden, shine on! Niki de Saint Phalle was a French-American who persisted despite those who lacked interest in showcasing her artwork of the true black Queen of California. Thanks to Ms. Niki, Queen Calafía is now rightfully placed from her mystical origins on the real ground of her namesake, California. For African, African American and Afro-Latino women, this is a significant royal, golden treasure -a chocolate gem interwoven in America! Now you have a reason to visit beautiful California. Educate and Celebrate!

---

[3] Garcí Rodriguez de Montalvo (GRM), "The Labors of the Very Brave Knight Esplandian" translated by William Thomas Little (1992).

ABOUT THE AUTHOR

"Tamra" from "Tamara" is Arabic for date of a palm tree. My parents named me after the first *California* superheroine actress Tamara Dobson. Queen Tamara played the lead in *Cleopatra Jones* films.

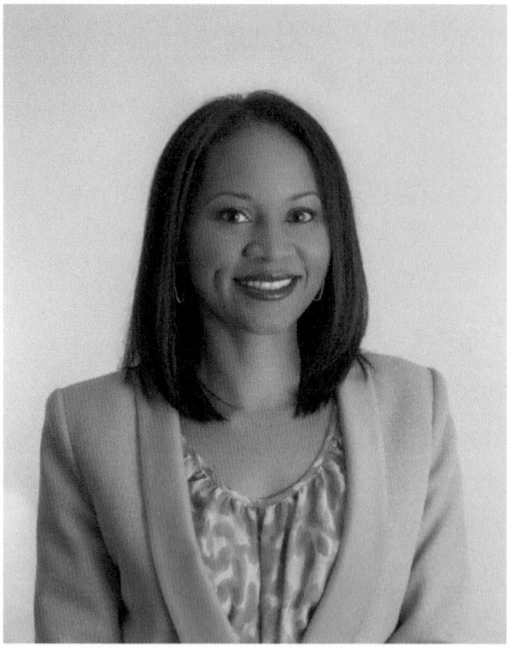

Tamra L. Dicus was born in Kansas City, Missouri, is an alumna of Tuskegee University, and spent her adult life in Alexandria, Virginia working for the USPTO and currently attends Thomas Jefferson School of Law, San Diego, California. Her experiences as a chemical engineer and patent examiner have mystically lead her to discover several facts of life upon her journey. She is founder and owner of CALIFORNIA IS ME EST. 1510®, established to concentrate on creating self-esteem in underrepresented youth, specifically on black women, and an overall, critical concentration in art, history, law, and STEM. Other upcoming projects: a book based on her mysterious collection of facts on her journey that lead her to discovery of Queen Calafía's California. Stay tuned for the book "Queen Calafía's X-facts". Ms. Dicus chose to celebrate her unknown "new black history" by creating empowering CALIFORINA IS ME EST. 1510™ fashionable clothing some of the designs in this book are available to wear! Explore, learn, and teach at: www.caliisme.com. Slay barriers in whatever you choose. President Obama slayed the political barrier twice by following in the steps of Shirley Chisholm, the first black, African American woman to become elected to U.S. Congress and run for president and from California (she displayed Calafía courage twice). History is full of strong courageous California warrior leaders; know you can do it too! Know that when something is obvious, you must state it, as what is not said is just as important too.

SOLVE THIS!

$$\sum_{k=C_t}^{\infty} \binom{n}{k^2} = [M^2 + B^2 + W^2]GPA$$

whereas

C_t = California Est. 1510

M=Mythical Majestic

B = Beautiful Black

W = Women Warriors

G= golden

P= passionate

A= Amazons

The next time you visit California Pizza Kitchen, think: "Strong, beautiful, courageous, Black women Amazons with gold weapons and griffins on a golden island" Pizza Kitchen.

Like the joy I felt when Obama won,
is the joy I hope when Calafía comes.
#Justice4QueenCalafia
#RevealTheSeal

#WonderQueenWarrior
#RealWonderWoman

#WQW
#RW2

You are the proof of California.

Queen Calafía is watching you!

APPENDIX

1526

Las fergas

dos teniã creydo que ꝺla muerte o ser capti
uos no podian escapar: porque ya vian los
suyos desmayados y heridos y los contra⸗
rios con grande esfuerço amenazãdo los cõ
crueles muertes: con crudas prisiones: con
aquella soberuia: cõ aq̃lla gloria: como si ya
en su poder los tuuiessen. Y el emperador co
mo quiera q̃ mucho esfuerço mostrasse: dan
do a todos esperãça de salud: su coraçõ muy
afligido ⁊ quebrantado era: temiendo siem⸗
pre enla memoria aq̃lla profecia que ya oy⸗
stes: viendo claramente como el efeto della
se yua cumpliẽdo. Assi se partierõ aq̃llos cõ
bates de aq̃l primero dia porq̃ la noche les
vino poniẽdo los paganos mucho recaudo
de nueua gẽte para en guarda ꝺ sus castillos
⁊ delos elefantes q̃ auiã quedado: ⁊ para no
perder ninguna cosa del sitio ꝺl campo que
auian ganado teniendo esperãça q̃ otro dia
llegarian sin peligro al pie dela cerca ⁊ la rõ
perian con sus artificios por tantas partes
q̃ muy de ligero podrian entrar y despachar
aquello que auian començado.

Capitulo.clxvj.

Como despues que mando dexar
Las puertas ẽ guarda ꝺ fuertes guerreros
El emperador y sus caualleros
Al grande palacio van reposar
E como las armas les hazen quitar
Aquellas señoras que tanto querian
Tintas de sangre segun que venian
Con mucho plazer se van a cenar.

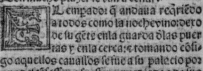

EL empador q̃ andaua req̃riẽdo
a todos como la noche vino: dexo
de su gẽte enla guarda ꝺlas puer
tas y enla cerca: ⁊ tomando cõsi⸗
go aquellos caualľos se fue a su palacio por
que descãsassen ⁊ fuessen remediados de sus
heridas. Y entrando cõ ellos enla sala hallo
que lo atendiã la emperatriz ⁊ su hija cõ sus
dueñas ⁊ dõzellas que ꝺsde que el combate
se començo nunca de su capilla se q̃taron las
rodillas hincadas en tierra rogando a dios
con muchas lagrimas que ouiesse merced ꝺ
los suyos. Assi fueron los caualľos por ellas
desarmados mas las espadas q̃ eran todas
teñidas ꝺ sangre hasta los puños siẽdo qua
jada enlas hinchadas manos nunca dellas
las pudierõ despegar sino con agua caliẽte.
Quitando los yelmos delas cabeças pares
cieron sus rostros hinchados: amanzillados
de aquellos grãdes golpes que les auiã da⸗
do: q̃ no por feos ꝺ aq̃llas señoras erã juzga
dos: mas por tã fermosos como las piedras
preciosas cõsiderando cõ q̃ esfuerço cõ q̃ va
lentia y cõ quã grãde afrenta y tã peligrosa
de sus vidas los auiã recebido. E luego les
fue dado ꝺ cenar: hablãdo el emperador cõ
ellos riendo delo que auian passado: loando
sus grandes cosas: y ellos diziendo le el grã
plazer que ouierõ de ver como los elefantes
bramauan y se reboluian cõ el olio q̃ ardien
do sobre ellos daua: y como al trastornar de
los castillos cayan los paganos las piernas
hazia arriba / ⁊ las cabeças abaxo vnos so⸗
bre otros q̃ en medio de su gran afrenta no
pudierõ escusar la risa. En esto que oys y en
otras muchas cosas passarõ la cena hasta q̃
se fueron a descansar q̃ biẽ les era menester.

Capit.clvij. del espanto⸗
so y no pensado socorro cõ que la reyna Ca
lafia en fauor delos turcos al puerto de con
stantinopla llego.

QUiero agora q̃ sepays vna cosa la
mas estraña que nũca por escriptu
ra ni por memoria de gente en nin⸗
gun caso hallar se pudo por donde
el dia siguiente fue la ciudad en punto de ser
perdida: ⁊ como de alli donde le vino el peli⸗
gro le vino la salud. Sabed q̃ ala diestra ma
no delas Indias vuo vna ysla llamada Ca
lifornia mucho llegada ala parte del paray⸗
so terrenal la qual fue poblada de mugeres
negras sin que algun varõ entre ellas ouies
se q̃ q̃si como las amazonas era su estilo ꝺ bi
uir estas erã de valientes cuerpos y esforça
dos y ardiẽtes coraçones ⁊ ꝺ grãdes fuerças.
La insula en si la mas fuerte de riscos ⁊ bra
uas peñas q̃ enel mũdo se hallaua. Las sus
armas erã todas de oro y tãbien las guarni
ciones delas bestias fieras en q̃ despues de
las auer amansado caualgauã que en toda
la ysla no auia otro metal alguno. Mora⸗
uan en cueuas muy bien labradas. Tenian

Excerpt of Garcí Rodríguez de Montalvo (GRM), Las fergas del muy virtuolo y effozcado cauallero Ef=plandianhijo de Alma=dis de Gaula, Bayerische Staatsbibliothek München, Germany, pg. 261, URN: bsb10197798, (1526).

redes estar a mi consejo. Todos aq̃llos grá
des señores le dixerõ q̃ como por ella fuesse
señalado q̃ assi lo mãdariã cũplir. Pues em
biad luego a todos los otros capitanes que
por ningũa manera salgan mañana ellos ni
los suyos de sus estanças hasta q̃ por mi les
sea mãdado ⁊ veres vn cõbate el mas estra
ño q̃ hasta oy nunca vistes: ni de q̃ jamas oy
stes hablar. Esto fue luego hecho saber al
grã soldã de liq̃a y al soldã de alapa q̃ tenian
cargo d̃ todas las huestes q̃ estauã enla tier
ra: los q̃les assi lo mandarõ a todas sus gen
tes marauillando se mucho a q̃ podria acu-
dir el pensamiento ⁊ obra de aq̃lla reyna.

Capitulo. clviij.

Como los grifos la gente q̃ vieron
En somo la cerca bolando lleuauan
Y muertos aquellos por otros tornauan
La mas fiera caça que hombres oyeron
E como los turcos que arriba subieron
Aquel mismo daño reciben penando
Los quales de grifo ayuda esperando
Por grifos la muerte cruel recibieron.

Passada aquella noche y la maña
na venida: la reyna Calafia sali
da d̃la mar: armada ella ⁊ sus mu
geres de aquellas armas de oro:
sembradas todas de piedras muy preciosas
que enla su insula de california como las pie
dras d̃l cãpo se hallauã segũ la su gran abun
dãcia: ⁊ puestas enlas bestias fieras guarne
cidas como vos diximos: mando abrir vna
puerta dela fusta donde los grifos venian.
Los q̃les como el cãpo vieron salieron todos cõ mucha priessa: mostrando gran plazer en bolar por el ayre. y desde vierõ la grã
gẽte q̃ por la cerca andaua como ellos ham
brientos estuuiessen: ⁊ sin ningũ temor cada
vno tomo el suyo en sus vñas ⁊ subiẽdo se en
alto comẽçarõ a comer enellos. Muchas
saetas les tirarõ: ⁊ muy grandes golpes les
dierõ cõ lãças ⁊ con espadas: mas su pluma
era tãta y tã junta ⁊ rezia q̃ nunca enla carne
les pudierõ tocar. Esta fue la mas hermosa
⁊ agradable caça ꝑa los de su ꝑte q̃ nũca vie
rõ hasta estõces. E como los turcos assi los
vierõ yr cõ sus enemigos bolãdo en alto: da
uan tan grandes bozes ⁊ alaridos de plazer
que el cielo foradauã: ⁊ la mas triste ⁊ mas
amargosa para los dela ciudad q̃ nunca ver
pudieron porque vian lleuar el padre al hijo
y el hijo al padre y al hermano y al pariẽte/
assi q̃ los llantos erã en tanto grado ⁊ las ra
uias q̃ por ellos haziã q̃ era grã cõpassiõ delos ver: despues q̃ los grifos anduuieron vn
espacio d̃ tpo por el ayre ⁊ auiẽdo soltado sus
p̄sas d̃llas enla mar ⁊ d̃llas enla tr̄ra torna-
rõ como d̃ cabo: ⁊ sin ningũ temor tomarõ o
tros tãtos d̃ q̃ los suyos ouierõ doblado pla
zer/ ⁊ los xp̄ianos muy mayor tristeza. Que
vos dire q̃ el espãto fue tã grande delos dela
cerca q̃ si no fueran algunos que se pusieron
enlas bouedas delas torres por alli guares
cer: de todos los otros fue desamparada: sin
q̃ ninguno en su defensa enella q̃dasse. Esto
visto por la reyna Calafia: dixo cõ vna boz
alta alos dos soldanes q̃ hiziessen a sus gen
tes subir por las escalas q̃ tomada era la ciu
dad. Estõces corrierõ todos a grã priessa/ ⁊
poniendo muchas escalas subieron sobre el
muro. Los grifos que ya auian soltado los
que lleuauan: como assi los vieron no teniẽdo ningũ conoscimiẽto dellos: tomaron los
por la manera q̃ alos xp̄ianos auiã fecho/ ⁊
bolãdo por el ayre los lleuaron hasta los de
xar caer dõde ningũo escapo d̃la muerte. A-
qui se troco el plazer y el pesar q̃ los d̃ fuera
auiẽdo grã piedad dellos llorauã. E los d̃ dẽ
tro teniẽdo se por vẽcidos: viẽdo alos enemi
gos andar por la cerca tomarõ en si muy grã
cõsuelo. A esta sazõ como los q̃ enel adarue
q̃darõ estuuiessen espãtados esperãdo d̃ mo
rir como sus cõpañeros. Salieron delas bo
uedas los xp̄ianos: y en poca de hora mata-
ron muchos delos turcos q̃ por la ronda ha
llaron: y alos otros hizieron saltar abaxo/ ⁊
tornaron se alas bouedas porque vian venir
los grifos hazia si. Quando aq̃llo fue visto
por la reyna Calafia fue muy triste en gran
manera: ⁊ dixo. Mis ydolos en quiẽ yo ado
ro ⁊ creo que sera esto: que assi es mi venida
fauorable a mis enemigos como a mis ami
gos: teniendo yo por creydo que con la vue-
stra ayuda ⁊ con mis fuertes compañas/ y
gran aparejo bastaua para su destruycion

Excerpt of Garcí Rodríguez de Montalvo (GRM), Las fergas del muy virtuolo y effozcado cauallero Ef=plandianhijo de Alma=dis de Gaula, Bayerische Staatsbibliothek München, Germany, pg. 264, URN: bsb10197798, (1526).

April 1862

45

THE NAME OF CALIFORNIA.

My attention was accidentally directed, a few weeks since, to what I think will prove the origin of the name of *California*, as applied to the peninsula so known. So far as I have seen, this account of the origin has escaped the attention of the historians; but I take the liberty to mention it to the Society, that I may ask if any of the chroniclers of California have alluded to it.

The name of California was given by Cortes, who discovered the peninsula in the year 1535. For the statement that he named it, we have the authority of Herrera.* It is proved, I think, that the expedition of Mendoza, in 1532, did not see California: it is certain that they gave it no name. Humboldt saw, in the archives of Mexico, a statement in manuscript, that it was discovered in 1526; † but for this there is

* Decade viii. book vi.

† It would be very desirable to have a new examination of the manuscript alluded to.

Excerpt of Edward E. Hale, *Proceedings of the American Antiquarian Society*, *The Name of California*, (Worcester, MA), April 30, 45, (1862).

Rev. Hale states that California's meaning has "[e]scaped the attention of the historians." Then he escalates his issue framed as a question (ignored for 157 years to date) to call attention, again. See Q9. Hale tries to prevent black women from being written out of American history.

March 1864

THE

ATLANTIC MONTHLY.

A MAGAZINE OF LITERATURE, ART, AND POLITICS.

VOL. XIII.—MARCH, 1864.—NO. LXXVII.

THE QUEEN OF CALIFORNIA.

I CAN see the excitement which this title arouses as it is flashed across the sierras, down the valleys, and into the various reading-rooms and parlors of the Golden City of the Golden State. As the San Francisco "Bulletin" announces some day, that in the "Atlantic Monthly," issued in Boston the day before, one of the articles is on "The Queen of California," what contest, in every favored circle of the most favored of lands, who the Queen may be! Is it the blond maiden who took a string of hearts with her in a leash, when she left us one sad morning? is it the hardy, brown adventuress, who, in her bark-roofed lodge, serves us out our boiled dog daily, as we come home from our water-gullies, and sews on for us weekly the few buttons which we still find indispensable in that toil? is it some Jessie of the lion-heart, heroine of a hundred days or of a thousand? is it that witch with gray eyes, cunningly bidden,—were they puzzled last night, or were they all wisdom crowded?—as she welcomed me, and as she bade me good-bye? Good Heavens! how many Queens of California are regnant this day! and of any one of them this article might be written.

No, *Señores!* No, *Caballeros!* Throng down to the wharves to see the Golden Era or the Cornelius's Coffin, or whatever other mail-steamer may bring these words to your longing eyes. Open to the right and left as Adams's express-messenger carries the earliest copy of the "Atlantic Monthly," sealed with the reddest wax, tied with the reddest tape, from the Corner Store direct to him who was once the life and light of the Corner Store, who now studies eschscholtzias through a telescope thirty-eight miles away on Monte Diablo! Rush upon the newsboy who then brings forth the bale of this Journal for the Multitude, to find that the Queen of California of whom we write is no modern queen, but that she reigned some five hundred and fifty-five years ago. Her precise contemporaries were Amadis of Gaul, the Emperor Esplandian, and the Sultan Radiaro. And she *flourished*, as the books say, at the time when this Sultan made his unsuccessful attack on the city of

---

Excerpt of Mr. Edward Everett Hale, *The Queen of California*, The Atlantic Monthly, March, 1864, 265-266. Courtesy of the Harvard University, Schlesinger Library, Boston, Mass.

Constantinople, — all of which she saw, part of which she was.

She was not *petite*, nor blond, nor golden-haired. She was large and black as the ace of clubs. But the prejudice of color did not then exist even among the most brazen-faced or the most copper-headed. For, as you shall learn, she was reputed the most beautiful of women; and it was she, O Californians, who wedded the gallant prince Talanque, — your first-known king. The supporters of the arms of the beautiful shield of the State of California should be, on the right, a knight armed *cap-à-pie*, and, on the left, an Amazon sable, clothed in skins, as you shall now see.

Mr. E. E. Hale, of Boston, sent to the Antiquarian Society last year a paper which shows that the name of California was known to literature before it was given to our peninsula by Cortés. Cortés discovered the peninsula in 1535, and seems to have called it California then. But Mr. Hale shows that twenty-five years before that time, in a romance called the "Deeds of Esplandian," the name of California was given to an island "on the right hand of the Indies." This romance was a sequel, or fifth book, to the celebrated romance of "Amadis of Gaul." Such books made the principal reading of the young blades of that day who could read at all. It seems clear enough, that Cortés and his friends, coming to the point farthest to the west then known,—which all of them, from Columbus down, supposed to be in the East Indies,—gave to their discovery the name, familiar to romantic adventurers, of *California*, to indicate their belief that it was on the "right hand of the Indies." Just so Columbus called his discoveries "the Indies,"—just so was the name "El Dorado" given to regions which it was hoped would prove to be golden. The romance had said, that in the whole of the romance-island of California there was no metal but gold. Cortés, who did not find a pennyweight of dust in the real California, still had no objection to giving so golden a name to his discovery.

Mr. Hale, with that brevity which becomes antiquarians, does not go into any of the details of the life and adventures of the Queen of California as the romance describes them. We propose, in this paper, to supply from it this reticency of his essay.

The reader must understand, then, that, in this romance, printed in 1510, sixty years or less after Constantinople really fell into the hands of the Turks, the author describes a pretended assault made upon it by the Infidel powers, and the rallying for its rescue of Amadis and Perion and Lisuarte, and all the princes of chivalry with whom the novel of "Amadis of Gaul" has dealt. They succeed in driving away the Pagans, "as you shall hear." In the midst of this great crusade, every word of which, of course, is the most fictitious of fiction, appear the episodes which describe California and its Queen.

First, of California itself here is the description : —

"Now you are to hear the most extraordinary thing that ever was heard of in any chronicles or in the memory of man, by which the city would have been lost on the next day, but that where the danger came, there the safety came also. Know, then, that, on the right hand of the Indies, there is an island called California, very close to the side of the Terrestrial Paradise,* and it was peopled by black women, without any man among them, for they lived in the fashion of Amazons. They were of strong and hardy bodies, of ardent courage and great force. Their island was the strongest in all the world, with its steep cliffs and rocky shores. Their arms were all of gold, and so was the harness of the wild beasts which they tamed and rode. For, in the whole island, there was no metal but gold. They lived in caves wrought

* When Columbus sailed on his fourth voyage, in which he hoped to pass through what we now know as the Isthmus of Panama, and sail northwestward, he wrote to his king and queen that thus he should come as near as men could come to "the Terrestrial Paradise."

Edward Everett Hale Courtesy of Harvard University fine arts c. 1857

Creditor for the etymology of California

CALIFORNIA IS ME

EST. 1510

"I am only one, but I am one. I cannot do everything. But I can do something. I will not let what I cannot do interfere with what I can do." — Dr. Rev. Edward Everett Hale

"[C]alifornia ... poblada de mujeres negras..."
— Garcí Rodríguez de Montalvo, Comic history innovator

"*She was not petite, nor blonde, nor golden-haired. She was large and black as the ace of clubs.*"
—Dr. Rev. Edward Everett Hale,
Harvard University graduate and Abolitionist

All *Hale* the Kings!

My Grade School Paper: "I'm Proud to be an American"

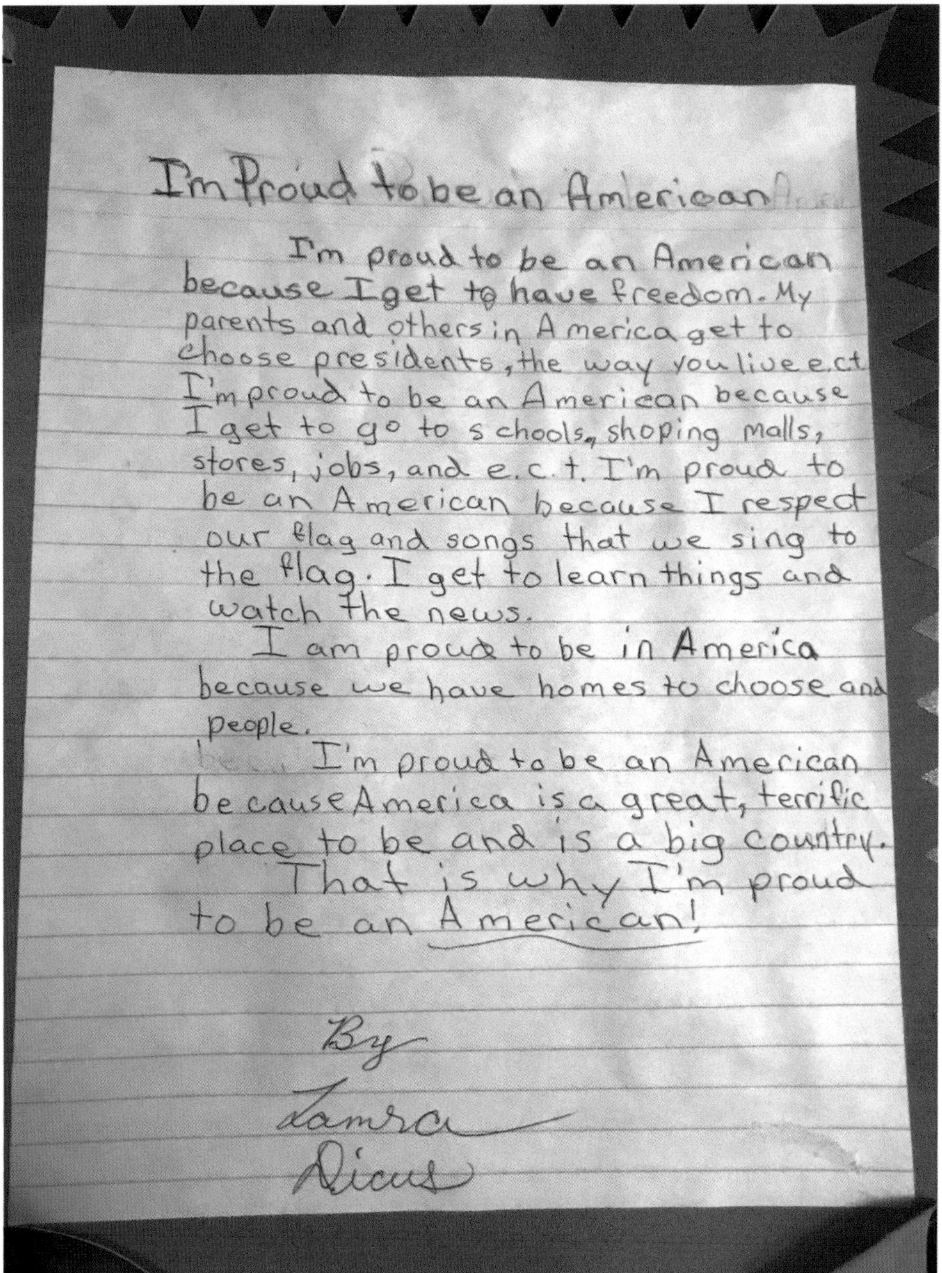

I'm Proud to be an American

I'm proud to be an American because I get to have freedom. My parents and others in America get to choose presidents, the way you live e.c.t I'm proud to be an American because I get to go to schools, shoping malls, stores, jobs, and e.c.t. I'm proud to be an American because I respect our flag and songs that we sing to the flag. I get to learn things and watch the news.

I am proud to be in America because we have homes to choose and people.

I'm proud to be an American because America is a great, terrific place to be and is a big country.

That is why I'm proud to be an American!

By
Tamra
Dicus

Thanks momma for having the
#BlackGirlMagic foresight
to save this!

I'm Proud to be an American Re-mix

I'm proud to be an American by way of California because I get to have freedom. Not just my body, but my mind too. My parents and others in America get to choose presidents, the way you live, etc. My parents and others in California get to choose assemblypersons, and the way you live, etc. Because California are all black women Amazons with golden weapons on a golden island, Black women inspired the quest for gold. Eventually the dream came true once one man really found gold for real! I am proud to be an American by way of California because I get to go to schools, shopping malls, stores, jobs and etc.

I'm proud to be an American by way of California because I respect our American flag and one day will dream of the time when the Black Queen Calafía and her queendom of California Black Women Amazons in the seal and flag look black like my grandma to me. Strongest, beautiful, courageous and powerful women.

I'm proud to be an American by way of California because I hope "we the people" can sing songs of liberty, one day for Queen Calafía will have justice. And I get to learn things and watch the news.

I'm proud to be an American by way of California because we have homes to choose and people to love. And one day I hope all will say thanks to my ancestors for the work they've done by fixing California. California Amazons taught me to fight for rights in America.

I'm proud to be an American by way of California because America is a great, terrific place to be and is a big country and California is a land of black magical golden dreams, and the biggest state in the land.

I am seen. I am apart of America after all! That is why I'm proud to be an American by way of California!

Think,
don't
peak.

TEACHING AID QUESTIONS

Q1: Who is the original creator of the Wonder Woman story and what was occurring world-wide in 1510 at the time in which *Las Sergas de Esplandían* was written? Why did Montalvo choose black women for the island of California?

Q2: Why is the time period surrounding the date of Dr. Rev. Hale's (1862 essay (see pg. 55) and 1864 article (pg. 56-57), important to publish for American history then?

Q3: Why is the time period in which Dr. Rev. Edward Everett Hale's articles, important to American history now (in the 21st century)?

Q4: Why would a Confederate general want to keep the California story in *Las Sergas* a secret during the American Civil War?

Q5: Why would today's *mujeres negras* (Black women) and all non-blacks across America want to know this unknown history today?

Q6: Did you know Ancient Greece and Rome moved into Ancient Egypt (of Nubian, dark, Black skin)? Did Hale know this? (See A6 and find the funny looking text. It is Grecian for "Eureka").

Q7: a) Would Black Hollywood have been affected? b) How can you become empowered? c) Why give credit to Calafía now? d) How do you feel knowing Calafía is not visible in the Great Seal?

Q8: Who are real life Black women queens from the past to today?

Q9: Why is California, still in the 21st century, not imaged in the "blackest of Egyptian marbles" (Hale, 1864 article)? Who hurts?

Q10: a) How did emancipated Sojourner Truth get her name? b) Would Truth, a victim of enslavement, if given an opportunity to read or vote, wanted to have known of Calafía's California?

Q11: Why would a *conquistador,* i.e. Cortes sail to the New World?

TEACHING AID ANSWERS

A1: Garcí Rodríguez de Montalvo. The Trans-Atlantic African Slave Trade. Arguably, Rodríguez de Montalvo cleverly wrote of inhumane, worldly treatment of the enslaved, equipped with superhero powers.

A2: Since 1492 Black women, men, and their children were enslaved throughout the Americas and Caribbean during the American Slave Trade. California entered statehood as a Union state in 1850. Yet, California's seal was designed in 1849 by a Confederate general. The period of the American Civil War was from 1861 to 1865. The Union stood for the abolition of Slavery (of body ***and*** mind). Thus, California should have followed suit upon entry. In 1863, President Abraham Lincoln further declared freedom of Slaves within the "rebellious states" in the Emancipation Proclamation. Prejudicially, a master native Virginian general, home to the Slaveholding State of the Confederacy, designed said seal (with a white queen not a black one) for a Union state. And CA "Powers" (see pg. 63) did not correct a deliberate error at entry or after. Rev. Hale returned an intellectual blow on behalf of abolitionists and the African Americans as they were forbidden to read during Slavery (as it was a crime to read).

A3: The Confederacy lost the Civil War; yet, we still glorify a losing entity. The name "California" is not accurately represented officially-anywhere. Diverse American citizens of whom would enjoy the true, Black Moor Spanish speaking woman leader and her monarchy of *California Amazonas* (aka wonder women) origins are prevented from our inalienable rights of enjoying the heritage as it is censored officially (in the flag when Nancy Pelosi, the first woman Speaker of the House, speaks on T.V.). Texas recently removed a Confederate plaque from its Capitol, so California can restore truth and stop propaganda.

A4: Control. Like Dr. King and Rosa Parks did for civil rights, Black women could have been inspired to fight for freedom on plantations.

A5: Africans, Black Americans and Afro-Latinas would feel pride that a Black woman's likeness and identity is uniquely, the namesake of the most popular state in the U.S.A. African baby names traditionally have meaning. By restoring the Nubian image, we can learn from its magical history.

A6: Hale knew Calafía is African; if drawing a goddess/queen, depict the Black Egyptian Nêith not a white Grecian Athena/Roman Minerva.

1864.] *The Queen of California.* 267

out of the rock with much labor. They had many ships with which they sailed out to other countries to obtain booty.

"In this island, called California, there were many griffins, on account of the great ruggedness of the country, and its infinite host of wild beasts, such as never were seen in any other part of the world. And when these griffins were yet small, the women went out with traps to take them. They covered themselves over with very thick hides, and when they had caught the little griffins, they took them to their caves, and brought them up there. And being themselves quite a match for the griffins, they fed them with the men whom they took prisoners, and with the boys to whom they gave birth, and brought them up with such arts that they got much good from them, and no harm. Every man who landed on the island was immediately devoured by these griffins; and although they had had enough, none the less would they seize them and carry them high up in the air, in their flight, and when they were tired of carrying them, would let them fall anywhere as soon as they died."

These griffins are the Monitors of the story, or, if the reader pleases, the Merrimacs. After this description, the author goes on to introduce us to our Queen. Observe, O reader, that, although very black, and very large, she is very beautiful. Why did not Powers carve his statue of California out of the blackest of Egyptian marbles? Try once more, Mr. Powers! We have found her now. Εὑρήκαμεν!

"Now at the time when those great men of the Pagans sailed with their great fleets, as the history has told you, there reigned in this island of California a Queen, very large in person, the most beautiful of all of them, of blooming years, and in her thoughts desirous of achieving great things, strong of limb and of great courage, more than any of those who had filled her throne before her. She heard tell that all the greater part of the world was moving in this onslaught against the Christians. She did not know what Christians were, for she had no knowledge of any parts of the world excepting those which were close to her. But she desired to see the world and its various people; and thinking, that, with the great strength of herself and of her women, she should have the greater part of their plunder, either from her rank or from her prowess, she began to talk with all of those who were most skilled in war, and told them that it would be well, if, sailing in their great fleets, they also entered on this expedition, in which all these great princes and lords were embarking. She animated and excited them, showing them the great profits and honors which they would gain in this enterprise, — above all, the great fame which would be theirs in all the world; while, if they stayed in their island, doing nothing but what their grandmothers did, they were really buried alive, — they were dead while they lived, passing their days without fame and without glory, as did the very brutes."

Now the people of California were as willing then to embark in distant expeditions of honor as they are now. And the first battalion that ever sailed from the ports of that country was thus provided: —

"So much did this mighty Queen, Calafia, say to her people, that she not only moved them to consent to this enterprise, but they were so eager to extend their fame through other lands that they begged her to hasten to sea, so that they might earn all these honors, in alliance with such great men. The Queen, seeing the readiness of her subjects, without any delay gave order that her great fleet should be provided with food, and with arms all of gold, — more of everything than was needed. Then she commanded that her largest vessel should be prepared with gratings of the stoutest timber; and she bade place in it as many as five hundred of these griffins, of which I tell you, that, from the time they were born, they were trained to feed on men. And she ordered that the beasts on which she and her people rode should be em-

Note: "Egypt" is the Grecian given name, originally named "Kem" or "Kemet".

In the 15th century, "Black women" meant African and those in "al-Andalus" -now named Spain. The flamenco dance was invented then.

Excerpt of Mr. Edward Everett Hale, *The Queen of California*, The Atlantic Monthly, March, 1864, 265-266. Courtesy of the Library of Congress, Washington, D.C. Microfilm

A7: "Swing Time": Black History = American History

a) Yes, for lack of roles. Black Hollywood suffered then and now. It's no secret that Hollywood has had a history of not casting Black people and when they did, the roles were stereotypical or done in blackface. Perhaps these truths disclosed herein serve to answer just why they have been reluctant to include Black people at Hollywood's inception. Note the 2017 *Wonder Woman* film debuted 76 years after the comic book (compared to only 40 years for Superman). See math on pg. 84 and Guinness World Records link: http://www.guinnessworldrecords.com/products/books/superlatives/superhero-timeline. To date, none of the history of Wonder Woman books identify Queen Calafía as the true, first comic (not the Black *sister* Nubia-cultural appropriation or creative license?). But in the first appearance of Nubia, Wonder Woman (vol. 1) #204, (January 1973), Wonder Woman speaks *Spanish* to *Nubia*! An obvious combination that directly originates in Mr. de Montalvo's *Sergas*. Now, Marvel's 2018 *Black Panther* portrays a California. b) Write to: Wonder Woman writers, social media (see pg. 69), sign the caliisme.com petition directed to the California assembly, or start a California parade. c) *E. pluburis unum*. Public tax funds are maintaining a Confederate designed seal. d) Jessica Dance, feels,

"To be completely transparent, I have mixed emotions. On one hand, it's a relief to know the truth and to be in the light while on the other hand, it is beyond disheartening to find out, yet again, that the truth is being kept from the Black community. Disheartening, but not shocking. Time after time, it appears that society continuously suppresses the Black community in one way shape or form and my question to those around us is why? Why are we oppressed? The Black woman is the backbone of many things in the United States yet it feels like time after time we, Black women, get the shorter end of the stick whether it be the truth being hidden from us, society portraying us as sexualized objects, being demonized as the "Angry Black Woman" whenever we express how we feel."

Note: On Chinese emigration and the California name, a CA newspaper stated: "There is neither justice, logic nor common sense in attempting to prejudice the minds of the American people on the merits of the Chinese question by a reference to the nets of a handful of criminals." The same can be said by simply substituting Chinese for African.

A8: "Remember the Time"

Africa's ancient indigenous queens are notably: Egyptian Queen Nefertiti, Egyptian Queen Mereneith, Egyptian Hatshepsut, Queen Amanirenas of the Nubian Kush Empire (land rich in gold and iron weaponry - is it not possible but probable because Calafía was an African Moor this empire in reality inspired art around Europe's Late Medieval Renaissance in Rodríguez de Montalvo's envisioned "California"?), Queen Asantewaa of the Ashanti Empire (now Ghana), Nigerian Queen Amina (Aminatu) Warrior Queen, Angolan Queen Njinga (Nzinga), and Ethiopian Queen Sheba. Did you know the George Washington monument looks like the ancient obelisks of Karnak, the palace of Queen Hatshepsut near Luxor (not Vegas)?

African American queen female leaders are notably: Unnamed slaves and ancestors, Sojourner Truth, Harriet Tubman, Septima Clark, Rosa Parks, Ida B. Wells, Dorothy Height, Shirley Chisholm, Madam C.J. Walker (*first* self-made *woman* millionaire), Katherine Johnson, Lena Horne, Mae Carole Jemison (first Black female to travel in space), Dorothy Dandridge, Halle Berry, Miriam Jiménez Román, Angela Davis, Aretha Franklin, Dr. Maya Angelou, Cathy Hughes, Whitney Houston, Condoleezza Rice, Maxine Waters, First Lady Michelle Obama, Kamala Harris (first Black U.S. Senator from California), Dr. Evelyn Brooks Higginbotham, Harvard University Director of History Department (first Black female to hold), Oprah Winfrey (first Black self-made woman billionaire), Misty Copeland (first Black principal ballerina), Venus and Serena Williams (aka Liota and Calafía), Gabby Douglas, Whoopi Goldberg, and Meghan Markle, Her Royal Highness the Duchess of Sussex- first ever Black American official British royalty: Queen of CA before UK duchess)!

If Black history has sparked your interest, read up and visit the Smithsonian's National African American History and Culture Museum in D.C. or any African American museum. When you learn world history and African regal history, it opens a door to African American identity (free and enslaved royalty) and the ways of the world. Know your worth. The future belongs to the youth. What world do you want to see? I saw myself in Wonder Woman. I hope all will see themselves in Queen Calafía, so she will no longer be invisible.

A9: **May 1864** Response by California Newspaper to Hale's Article

6 SACRAMENTO DAILY UNION, MONDAY, MAY 2, 1864.

SACRAMENTO DAILY UNION.

SONG FROM "SUPPER AT THE MILL."

BY JEAN INGELOW.

When sparrows build, and the leaves break forth,
My old sorrow wakes and cries,
For I know there is dawn in the far, far North,
And a scarlet sun doth rise;
Like a scarlet fleece the snow fields spread,
And the ice founts run free,
And the bergs begin to bow their heads,
And plunge and sail in the sea.

Oh, my lost love, and my own, own love,
And my love that loved me so!
Is there never a chink in the world above
Where they listen for words from below?
Nay, I spoke once, and I grieved thee sore,
I remember all that I said,
And now thou wilt hear me no more—no more
Till the sea gives up her dead.

Thou did'st set thy foot on the ship, and sail
To the ice fields and the snow;
Thou wert sad, for thy love did not avail,
And the end I could not know.
How could I tell I should love thee to-day,
Whom that day I held not dear?
How could I know I should love thee away,
When I did not love thee anear?

We shall walk no more through the sodden plain
With the faded bents o'erspread;
We shall stand no more by the seething main,
While the dark wrack drives o'erhead;
We shall part no more in the wind and rain,
Where thy last farewell was said;
But perhaps I shall meet thee and know thee again
When the sea gives up her dead.

THE QUEEN OF CALIFORNIA.

[From the Atlantic Monthly.]

The Queen of California of whom we write is no modern queen; she reigned some five hundred and fifty-five years ago. Her precise contemporaries, were Amadis of Gaul, the Emperor Esplandian, and the Sultan Radiaro. And she flourished, as the books say, at the time when this Sultan made his unsuccessful attack on the city of Constantinople—all of which she saw, part of which she was.

She was not *petite*, nor blond, nor golden-haired. She was large and black as the ace of clubs. But the prejudice of color did not then exist, even among the most brazen-faced, or the most copper-headed. For, as you shall learn, she was reputed the most beautiful of women; and it was she, O Californians, who wedded the gallant Prince Talanque—your first known king. The supporters of the arms of the beautiful shield of the State of California should be, on the right, a knight armed *cap-a-pie*, and on the left, an Amazon sable, clothed in skins, as you shall now see.

E. E. Hale, of Boston, sent to the Antiquarian Society, last year, a paper which shows that the name of California was known to literature be-

without fame and without glory, as did the very brutes."

Now the people of California were as willing then to embark in distant expeditions of honor as they are now. And the first battalion that ever sailed from the ports of that country was thus provided:

"So much did this mighty Queen, Calafia, say to her people, that she not only moved them to consent to this enterprise, but they were so eager to extend their fame through other lands that they begged her to hasten to sea, so that they might earn all these honors, in alliance with such great men. The Queen, seeing the readiness of her subjects, without any delay gave orders that her great fleet should be provided with food and with arms of gold—more of everything than was needed. Then she commanded that her largest vessel should be prepared with gratings of the stoutest timber; and she bade place in it as many as five hundred of these griffins, of which I tell you, that, from the time they were born, they were trained to feed on men. And she ordered that the beasts on which she and her people rode should be embarked, and all the best-armed women and those most skilled in war whom she had in her island. And then, leaving such force in the island that it should be secure, with the others she went to sea. And they made such haste that they arrived at the fleets of the Pagans the night after the battle of which I have told you; so that they were received with great joy, and the fleet was visited at once by many great Lords, and they were welcomed with great acceptance. She wished to know at once in what condition affairs were, asking many questions, which they answered fully. Then she said

"'You have fought this city with your great forces, and you cannot take it; now, if you are willing, I wish to try what my forces are worth to-morrow, if you will give orders accordingly.'

"All these great lords said that they would give such commands as she should bid them.

"'Then send word to all your other captains that they shall to-morrow on no account leave their camps, they nor their people, until I command them; and you shall see a combat more remarkable than you have ever seen or heard of.'

"Word was sent at once to the great Sultan of Liquia and the Sultan of Halapa, who had command of all the men who were there; and they gave these orders to their people, wondering much what was the thought of this Queen."

Up to this moment, it may be remarked, these Monitors, as we have called the griffins, had never been fairly tried in any attack on fortified towns. The Dupont of the fleet, whatever her name may have been, may well have looked with some curiosity on the issue. The experiment was not wholly successful, as will be seen.

"When the night had passed and the morn-

"Exhortation addressed by the author to the Christians, setting before their eyes the great obedience which these griffins, brute animals, rendered to those who had instructed them."

The Sultans may have well doubted whether their new ally was quite what she had claimed to be. She felt this herself, and said to them:

"'Since my coming has caused you so much injury, I wish that it may cause you equal pleasure. Command your people, that they shall sally out, and we will go to the city against those knights who dare to appear before us, and we will let them press on the most severe combat that they can, and I, with my people, will take the front of the battle.'

"The Sultans gave command at once to all of their soldiers who had armor, that they should rush forth immediately, and should join in mounting upon the rampart, now that these birds were encaged again. And they, with the horsemen, followed close upon Queen Calafia, and immediately the army rushed forth and pressed upon the wall; but not so prosperously as they had expected, because the people of the town were already there in their harness, and as the Pagans mounted upon their ladders, the Christians threw them back, whence very many of them were killed and wounded. Others pressed forward with their iron picks and other tools, and dug fiercely in the circuit of the wall. These were very much distressed and put in danger by the oil and other things which were thrown upon them, but not so much but that they succeeded in making many breaches and openings. But when this came to the ears of the Emperor, who always kept command of ten thousand horsemen, he commanded all of them to defend these places as well as they could. So that, to the grief of the Pagans, the people repaired the breaches with many timbers and stones and piles of earth.

"When the Queen saw this repulse she rushed with her own attendants with great speed to the gate Aquilena, which was guarded by Norandel.* She herself went in advance of the others, wholly covered with one of those shields which we have told you they wore, and with her lance held strongly in her hand. Norandel, when he saw her coming, went forth to meet her, and they met so vehemently that their lances were broken in pieces, and yet neither of them fell. Norandel at once put hand upon his sword, and the Queen upon her great knife, of which the blade was more than a palm broad, and they gave each other great blows. At once they all joined in a melee, one against another, all so confused and with such terrible blows that it was a great marvel to see it; and if some of the women fell upon the ground, so did some of the cavaliers. And if this history does not tell in extent which of them fell, and by what blow of

gained by us, whence it will be clearly seen in the future how the victory will be on our side."

This challenge was taken to the Christian camp by a black and beautiful damsel, richly attired, and was discussed there in council. Amadis put an end to the discussion by saying—

"'My good Lords, as the affairs of men, like those of nations, are in the hands and will of God, whence no one can escape but as He wills, if we should in any way withdraw from this demand, it would give great courage to our enemies, and, more than this, great injury to our honor, especially so in this country, where we are strangers, and no one has seen what our power is, which in our own land is notorious, so that, while there we may be esteemed for courage, here we should be judged the greatest of cowards. Thus, placing confidence in the mercy of the Lord, I determine that the battle shall take place without delay.'

"'If this is your wish,' said King Lisuarte and King Perion, 'so may it be, and may God help you with His grace!'

"Then the King Amadis said to the damsel:

"'Friend, tell your lord and the Queen Calafia that we desire the battle with those arms that are the most agreeable to them; that the field shall be this field, divided in the middle, I giving my word that for nothing which may happen will we be succored by our own. And let them give the same order to their own; and if they wish the battle now, now it shall be.'

"The damsel departed with this reply, which she repeated to those two princes. And the Queen Calafia asked her how the Christians appeared.

"'Very nobly,' replied she, 'for they are all handsome and well armed. Yet I tell you, Queen, that among them this Knight of the Serpent [Esplandian, son of Amadis] is such as neither the past nor the present, nor, I believe, any who are to come, have ever seen one so handsome and so elegant, nor will see in the days which are to be. O, Queen, what shall I say to you but that, if he were of our faith, we might believe that our gods had made him with their own hands, with all their power and wisdom, so that he lacks in nothing?'

"The Queen, who heard her, said:

"'Damsel, my friend, your words are too great.'

"'It is not so,' said she; 'for, excepting the sight of him, there is nothing else which can give account of his great excellence.'

"'Then I say to you,' said the Queen, 'that I will not fight with such a man until I have first seen and talked with him; and I make this request to the Sultan, that he will gratify me in this thing, and arrange that I may see him.'

"The Sultan said,

"'I will do everything, O Queen, agreeably

hand, she permitted them to help upon her strange steed."

At this point the novel assume high virtue (*virtus*, mannishness, the more brutal sex) on the woman's rights, in especial of wome fight in the field with gold armor, h and casque closed. We will show t she follows us, how careful she must island of the sea which has been sli known by the last five centuries, s pen to meet a cavalier of the tru chivalry.

Esplandian himself would not in lute the Queen Calafia as she lef was this a Copperhead prejudice o that prejudice was not yet known.

"He made no reply to her, both looked at her as something stran beautiful she appeared to him, and saw her come thus in arms, so differ style in which a woman should hav he considered it as very dishonora should attempt anything so differe the word of God commanded her, man should be in subjection to t rather should prefer to be the ruler not by her courtesy, but by force of above all, because he hated to plac relations with her, because she wa infidels whom he mortally despis taken a vow to destroy."

The romance then goes into an ac preparations for the contest on both

After all the preliminaries we "they separated for a little, and r furiously in full career. The Sulta plandian in the shield with so hard a part of the lance passed throu much as an ell, so that all who sa that it had passed through the body. not so, but the lance passed under t the body, and went out on the oth out touching him. But Esplandian, that his much-loved lady was lookin norina, the daughter of the Emp stantinople], so struck the Sultan's the iron passed through it and str some of the strongest plates of his which the spear turned. But, with the encounter, it shook him so r the saddle that it rolled him upon and so shook the helmet as to tear his head, and thus Esplandian pa very handsomely, without receiving himself. The Queen rushed upon he upon her, and, before they met, lance at the other, and they receive upon their shields in such guise th flew in pieces, while that of Amadi and was thrown on one side. The met, shield to shield, with such fo

Above and below (enlarged) excerpt of *The Queen of California [From the Atlantic Monthly],* Sacramento Daily Union, May 2, 1864, at 6.

These griffins are the Monitors of the story, or, if the reader pleases, the Merrimacs. After this description, the author goes on to introduce to us our Queen. Observe, O reader, that, although very black and very large, she is very beautiful. Why did not Powers carve his statue of California out of the blackest of Egyptian marbles? Try once more, Powers! We have found her now.

"Now, at the time when those great men of the pagans sailed with their great fleets, as the history has told you, there reigned in this island of California a Queen, very large in person, the most beautiful of all of them, of blooming

A slight war of words during the Civil War commences in just two months after the Atlantic Monthly published Hale's article. *Note*: 1) The headline states, "From the Atlantic Monthly", but the beginning of Hale's article is omitted (see pg. 56) and thus is an incomplete copy; and 2) the critical Grecian text was omitted (see A6). Another CA newspaper later changed the spelling to "Califia", and drew a false white, not black queen. Propaganda. One cannot fix what one cannot see. Suppressing positive black history hurts the race at birth, the public, legacy of Lincoln, US colored troops/veterans.

Note: the AFRO newspaper article: The Real Meaning of California is #BlackGirlMagic explains just why the issue is being swept under the rug, kicking the can down the road of history over a well settled issue. Hint: race/power.

A10: **April 1863** Freed Truth reclaimed her name; See column 2.

478 *Sojourner Truth, the Libyan Sibyl.* [April,

was holdin' a court, to see ef I could find any grand jury. An' I stood round the court-house, an' when they was a-comin' out, I walked right up to the grandest-lookin' one I could see, an' says I to him, —

"'Sir, be you a grand jury?'

"An' then he wanted to know why I asked, an' I told him all about it; an' he asked me all sorts of questions, an' finally he says to me, —

"'I think, ef you pay me ten dollars, that I 'd agree to git your son for you.' An' says he, pointin' to a house over the way, 'You go 'long an' tell your story to the folks in that house, an' I guess they 'll give you the money.'

"Well, I went, an' I told them, an' they gave me twenty dollars; an' then I thought to myself, 'Ef ten dollars will git him, twenty dollars will git him *sartin*.' So I carried it to the man all out, an' said, —

"'Take it all, — only be sure an' git him.'

"Well, finally they got the boy brought back; an' then they tried to frighten him, an' to make him say that I was n't his mammy, an' that he did n't know me; but they could n't make it out. They gave him to me, an' I took him an' carried him home; an' when I came to take off his clothes, there was his poor little back all covered with scars an' hard lumps, where they 'd flogged him.

"Well, you see, honey, I told you how I prayed the Lord to render unto her double. Well, it came true; for I was up at ole missis' house not long after, an' I heerd 'em readin' a letter to her how her daughter's husband had murdered her, — how he 'd thrown her down an' stamped the life out of her, when he was in liquor; an' my ole missis, she giv a screech, an' fell flat on the floor. Then says I, 'O Lord, I did n't mean all that! You took me up too quick.'

"Well, I went in an' tended that poor critter all night. She was out of her mind, — a-cryin', an' callin' for her daughter; an' I held her poor ole head on my arm, an' watched for her as ef she 'd been my babby. An' I watched by her, an' took care on her all through her sickness after that, an' she died in my arms, poor thing!"

"Well, Sojourner, did you always go by this name?"

"No, 'deed! My name was Isabella; but when I left the house of bondage, I left everything behind. I wa'n't goin' to keep nothin' of Egypt on me, an' so I went to the Lord an' asked Him to give me a new name. And the Lord gave me Sojourner, because I was to travel up an' down the land, showin' the people their sins, an' bein' a sign unto them. Afterwards I told the Lord I wanted another name, 'cause everybody else had two names; and the Lord gave me Truth, because I was to declare the truth to the people.

"Ye see some ladies have given me a white satin banner," she said, pulling out of her pocket and unfolding a white banner, printed with many texts, such as, "Proclaim liberty throughout all the land unto all the inhabitants thereof," and others of like nature. "Well," she said, "I journeys round to camp-meetins, an' wherever folks is, an' I sets up my banner, an' then I sings, an' then folks always comes up round me, an' then I preaches to 'em. I tells 'em about Jesus, an' I tells 'em about the sins of this people. A great many always comes to hear me; an' they 're right good to me, too, an' say they want to hear me agin."

We all thought it likely; and as the company left her, they shook hands with her, and thanked her for her very original sermon; and one of the ministers was overheard to say to another, "There 's more of the gospel in that story than in most sermons."

Sojourner stayed several days with us, a welcome guest. Her conversation was so strong, simple, shrewd, and with such a droll flavoring of humor, that the Professor was wont to say of an evening, "Come, I am dull, can't you get Sojourner up here to talk a little?" She would come up into the parlor, and sit among pictures

Excerpt of Stowe, Harriet Beecher. "Sojourner Truth, The Libyan Sibyl." The Atlantic Monthly 11, no. 66 (April 1863): 473-482. Courtesy of the Library of Congress, Washington, D.C. Microfilm

a) "My name was Isabella; but when I left the house of bondage; I wa'n't goin' to keep nothin' of Egypt on me, an' so I went to the Lord an' asked Him to give me a new name. And the Lord gave me Sojourner, because I was to travel up an' down the land, showin' the people their sins, an' bein' a sign unto them. Afterwards I told the Lord I wanted... another name, 'cause everybody else had two names.; and the Lord gave me Truth, because I was to declare the truth to the people." b) Her name says it all.

A11: **1859** Hernan Cortez's Fountain of Youth

Author Farnham is stunned that:

> [T]his Cortez, in 1524, believes in a nation of immense women, called Amazons, inhabiting a very large island whose shores are strewn with pearls and gold! . . . Cortez determines to discover the habitation of these large ladies. But in 1528 his fame falls into the hands of Spaniards who treat it with the same respect as they already have that of Columbus; that is, begin to dig its grave. To avoid the vexations which the Viceroy of Mexico, and a few other envious men, . . . [h]e sails to Spain and presents himself to his King. He is received at court . . .[m]ade . . .[C]aptain General of New Spain . . .[d]iscoverer and people of those coasts and of the island of pearls, gold, and Amazons.

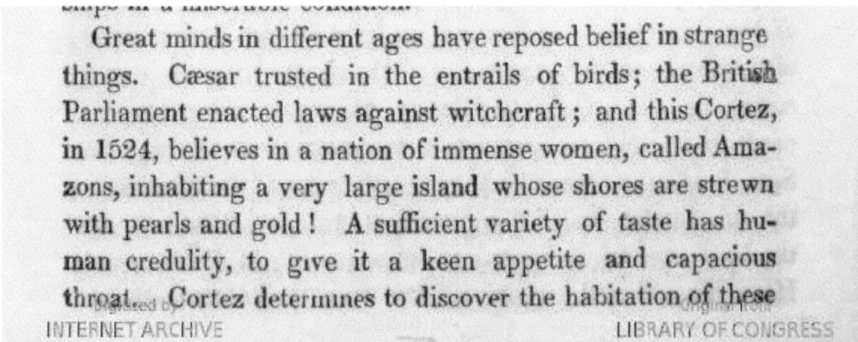

Great minds in different ages have reposed belief in strange things. Cæsar trusted in the entrails of birds; the British Parliament enacted laws against witchcraft; and this Cortez, in 1524, believes in a nation of immense women, called Amazons, inhabiting a very large island whose shores are strewn with pearls and gold! A sufficient variety of taste has human credulity, to give it a keen appetite and capacious throat. Cortez determines to discover the habitation of these

Excerpt from J. T. Farnham, esq./Farnham, Thomas Jefferson, The Early Days of California : Embracing What I Saw And Heard There, With Scenes in the Pacific. 1804-1848, 120-121, (Philadelphia, J.E. Potter, 1859). Courtesy of Library of Congress, Washington, D.C.

It is AMAZING how the large Amazon ladies on a gold island from the *Sergas* novel has traveled in time. Power to the pen! "The Columbian Exchange" included goods, including slaves, to trade in America. Free Blacks also came such as the first wheat cultivator in the Americas, Juan Garrido.

1562 *Americae sive quartae orbis partis nova et exactissima descriptio* map

Source: Library of Congress, Washington, D.C. Gutiérrez, Diego, 1554-1569, Americae sive qvartae orbis partis nova et exactissima descriptio / avctore Diego Gvtiero Philippi Regis Hisp. etc. Cosmographo ; Hiero. Cock excvde. 1562 ; Hieronymus Cock excude cum gratia et priuilegio 1562, [Antwerp : s.n.], 1562. Map

Do you see "C California" in the first drawn map of America?

Think: Would you like your essence or contributions erased away or ignored or whitewashed? If Justin Bieber was painted Black in the future, how would you feel? President Barack Obama's image is in jeopardy 100 years from now if we don't fix this. While artistry is in the eyes of the beholder, it rides a fine line of ignoring diverse attributes if it erases major contributions of a race of people during the quest for creativity. It is unethical, especially in government (i.e. power = **we** the people). Give credit where credit is due. We command our first official seal bearing a black face. Celebrate with a selfie or spread the word. Email queenc@caliisme.com subject: selfie

THE NAME OF CALIFORNIA.

My attention was accidentally directed, a few weeks since, to what I think will prove the origin of the name of *California*, as applied to the peninsula so known. So far as I have seen, this account of the origin has escaped the attention of the historians; but I take the liberty to mention it to the Society, that I may ask if any of the chroniclers of California have alluded to it.

The name of California was given by Cortes, who discovered the peninsula in the year 1535. For the statement that he named it, we have the authority of Herrera.* It is proved, I think, that the expedition of Mendoza, in 1532, did not see California: it is certain that they gave it no name. Humboldt saw, in the archives of Mexico, a statement in manuscript, that it was discovered in 1526; † but for this there is

---

* Decade viii. book vi.

† It would be very desirable to have a new examination of the manuscript alluded to.

no other authority. It is certain that the name does not appear till 1535.

No etymology of this name has been presented, satisfactory to the historians. Venegas,* the Jesuit historian of California, writing in 1758, sums up the matter in these words: —

"The most ancient name is California, used by Bernal Dias, limited to a single bay. I could wish to gratify the reader by the etymology and true origin of this name; but in none of the various dialects of the natives could the missionaries find the least traces of such a name being given by them to the country, or even to any harbor, bay, or small part of it. Nor can I subscribe to the etymology of some writers, who suppose the name to be given to it by the Spaniards, on their feeling an unusual heat at their first landing here; that they thence called the country *California*, compounding the two Latin words *calida* and *fornax*, 'a hot furnace.' I believe few will think the adventurers could boast of so much literature."

I believe the Californian authors of our own time agree with Venegas in rejecting this forced etymology. The word to be made from it should be "Calidafornacia." Dr. Bushnell, who says the heat of the interior valleys is that of a baker's furnace, speaks of a region which Cortes never saw. It must be recollected, that, though Bernal Dias only uses the name for the bay, we have Herrera's better authority for saying that Cortes saw it to the peninsula. But

* The work of Venegas is chiefly due to the labors of Father Andres Marcos Buriel, according to Greenhow.

neither peninsula nor bay is the oven described by Dr. Bushnell.

Clavigero, in his "History of California," after giving this etymology, offers as an alternative the following, as the opinion "of the learned Jesuit, D. Giuseppe Compoi:" "He believes that the name is composed of the Spanish word *cala*, which means 'a little cove of the sea;' and the Latin *fornix*, which means 'the vault of a building.'" He thinks these words are thus applied, "because, within Cape St. Lucas, there is a little cove of the sea, towards the western part of which rises a rock, so worn out, that on the upper part of the hollow is seen a vault, as perfect as if made by art. Cortes, therefore, observing this *cala*, or cove, and this vault, probably called this port *California*, or *cala* and *fornix;* speaking half in Spanish, half in Latin."

Clavigero suggests, as an improvement on this somewhat wild etymology, that Cortes may have said *Cala fornax*, "Cove furnace;" speaking, as in the Jesuit's suggestion, in two languages.

I am told that the Rev. Dean Trench, in one of his etymological works, suggests the Greek καλή πορνεία, — implying that the province seemed to the early settlers to have the attractions of a "beautiful adultery." I have not myself found this passage: but I remember that Mr. Powers, the sculptor, represents California as a naked woman, seductive in front, but concealing a thorn bush in her hands behind; and he describes his statue as intended to represent her false seductions. Of this etymology, it is enough to say, that Cortes and his men knew nothing of the seductions, — never finding gold or any thing else tempting there; and that the theory requires more, yet worse, scholarship at their hands than that of *calida fornax*.

Of all such speculations, Mr. Greenhow says very fitly, "None of them are satisfactory, or even ingenious."

It is in the worthless romance of the "Sergas of Esplandian," the son of Amadis of Gaul, — a book long since deservedly forgotten, — that there is to be found, I believe, the source from which the adventurers transferred the name "California" to the new region of their discovery.

Towards the close of this romance, the various Christian knights assemble to defend the Emperor of the Greeks and the city of Constantinople against the attacks of the Turks and Infidels. On this occasion, in a romance published first in 1510, — twenty-five years before Cortes discovered the American California, — the name appears, with precisely our spelling, in the following passage: —

Sergas, ch. 157. — "Know that, on the right hand of the Indies, there is an island called California, very near to the Terrestrial Paradise, which was peopled with black women, without any men among them, because they were accustomed to live after the fashion of Amazons. They were of strong and hardened bodies, of ardent courage, and of great force. The island was the strongest in the world, from its steep rocks and great cliffs. Their arms were all of gold; and so were the caparisons of the wild beasts which they rode, after having tamed them: for in all the island there is no other metal. They lived in caves very well worked out; they had many ships, in which they sailed to other parts to carry on their forrays. . . .

"In this island, called California, are many griffins, on account of the great savageness of the country, and the immense quantity of wild game to be found there. . . .

"Now, in the time that those great men of the Pagans sailed [against Constantinople] with those great fleets of which I have told you, there reigned in this Island of California a queen, very large of body, very beautiful, in the prime of her years, desirous to achieve great things; strong, brave, eager, and of good courage, — more than any of those who had before this held her kingdom. And, hearing tell how the greater part of the world was moving against the Christians, not knowing what sort of thing the Christians were, and having no knowledge of other countries but those which were near her own; desiring to see the world and its various races; thinking that, with the great power which she and her people could bring, of all that they gained, she would, from her strength and rank, obtain the greater part, — she talked with all those who were skilful in war, and told them that it would be well, if, embarking in their greatest fleets, they followed in the way in which so many great princes and lords were following. Animating and encouraging them, she set before them the great honors and inducements which such a course offered them; above all, showing them how much more fame they would gain through all the world than if they remained in this island, where, doing only what their grandmothers did, they were only buried alive, — living like those who were dead; passing their days, without fame or glory, as the brute beasts do."

By these persuasions, she induces them to join in the attack on Constantinople; and they sail with fifty griffins, to act as a sort of flying armored squadron under their orders.

The name of this queen is Calafia. Arrived at the war, she fights with Norandel, the brother of Amadis; and afterwards, being overcome by the great hero Amadis himself, she is taken prisoner. In the Christian court, she is converted to Christianity, and marries Talanque, nephew of Amadis, and son of Galaor; with whom she goes back to California, promising to abolish its Amazonian customs. The griffins prove poor allies; preferring to attack the naked Turks, and leaving the Greeks in their armor.

The name "California" thus appears in several distinct passages in the history.

This romance, as I have said, is believed to have been printed first in 1510. No copies of this edition, however, are extant. But, of the edition of 1519, a copy is preserved: and there are copies of successive editions of 1521, 1525, and 1526; in which last year, two editions were published, — one at Seville, and the other at Burgos. All of these are Spanish.

It follows, almost certainly, that Cortes and his followers, in 1535, must have been acquainted with the romance; and, as they sailed up the west side of Mexico, they supposed they were precisely at the place indicated, — "in the right hand of the Indies." It will be remembered also, that, by sailing in the same direction, Columbus, in his letter to the sovereigns, says "he shall be sailing towards the Terrestrial Paradise." We need not suppose that Cortes believed the romance, more than we do; though we assert that he borrowed a name from it to indicate the peninsula he found "on the right side of the Indies, near to the Terrestrial Paradise." If it is necessary to analyze very carefully his motive for borrowing a name from a romance then so generally known, it will be enough to say, that this romance credited the "Island of California" with great treasures of gold; and that it placed it very near the East Indies, in quest of which all the adventurers of that time were sailing. There is, however, no more reason for giving a serious motive for such a nomenclature, than there is for the motive with which La Salle or his companions gave the name of La Chine to the point in Canada from which they hoped to reach China.

It is not strange that ecclesiastical historians, like Venegas, should, in the eighteenth century, have lost sight of this origin of the name. It was not until 1683 that the Jesuit fraternity succeeded in planting an establishment there. Even then, their establishment was not permanent. For a century and a half, therefore, after Cortes's discovery, the province was of no value to any one, and its name was of as little interest. Long before the Jesuits planted it, the romance which gave it name was forgotten.

After 1542, no edition of the "Sergas of Esplandian" was printed in Spain, so far as we know, till 1575;

and, after that of 1587, none for two hundred and seventy years more. The re-action had come. When the curate burned the books of Don Quixote, he burned this among the rest: he saved "Amadis of Gaul," but he burned "Esplandian." "We will not spare the son," said he, "for the virtues of his father." These words show Cervantes's estimate of it as early as 1605. It is not surprising, then, that an ecclesiastic like Venegas should not know, in 1758, the wild geography of the romance two centuries and more after it was written. D'Herbelay, the early French paraphraser of this romance, retains the whole story of the queen, but transfers the situation of California to the source of the river Borysthenes, near the descent of the Riphean Mountains.

The only effort to introduce it to modern readers, in any European country, until the recent Spanish reprint of 1857, is in the wretched paraphrase by Tressan, published in France in the last century. This author, as if to add to the probability of the tale, omits the name "California" in each of the passages relating to it; so that, even in his forgotten work, we do not get hold of the lost clew.

The original work is now so rare, that I think the copies in the valuable library of Mr. Ticknor are the only ones in Massachusetts. To his invaluable collection, and to that kind courtesy which opens it to every student, and illustrates it from the treasures of his own studies, am I indebted for all the authorities of value which I am able to cite here. There is no copy of the "Esplandian" in our leading public libraries. In the large public libraries of the city of New York, there is no copy of any of these romances, which made the lay literature of the first century after printing was invented; but in the small yet well-selected library of the Free Academy of New York, and in that of Congress, I found the "Amadis" and "Esplandian," in the recent Spanish edition, edited by D. Pascal de Gayangos.

The "Esplandian" was written by Garcia Ordoñez de Montalvo, the translator of the "Amadis." In ascribing to it the origin of the name "California," I know that I furnish no etymology for that word. I have not found the word in any earlier romances. I will only suggest, that the root *Calif*, the Spanish spelling for the sovereign of the Mussulman power of the time, was in the mind of the author as he invented these Amazon allies of the Infidel power.

EDWARD E. HALE.

LAST THOUGHTS

Since stripped of our African names, "California" is the only African American name we have. Being Black matters in the Olympics as a distinct race with celebratory cheers; yet is censored officially in a state seal (maintained by a few clueless taxpayers). Exploitation of African Americans is valued more than officially correcting the history (even when it is right to do so). I surprisingly saw for myself how import African American imagery was when I traveled to Nigeria. I saw so many products and monetary notes with black faces on them. People were laughing at me because I kept taking pictures of Colgate® toothpaste bearing black faces. I had not seen that in America since; thankfully, a slight shift occurred. Cultural shifts will continue by educating youth on character, civility and history. We can eradicate racism, colorism, sexism, bullying, etc. And so, I refer again to my good friend Jessica Dance, J.D. TJSL:

> One word, truth. . . And it is also true that, many truths are concealed from we, the people. And so, what does this mean? . . .[I]t is not a shock to the conscious that certain races (and other groups) are portrayed a certain way in society, more specifically Black women are negatively portrayed as being sexual, lazy, angry, etc. For those of you who may not be able to relate to being a Black woman, you may relate to feeling like you're placed in a categorical box and unable to escape because of your race, gender, sexuality, political beliefs, religious beliefs, national origin, disability, etc. . . The truth is, the stereotypes of Black women are not indicative of all Black women as evidenced by Tamra Dicus' dedication, Michelle Obama's achievements, Oprah Winfrey's accomplishments, Kamala Harris' tenacity, Kerry Washington's drive. . .What is the truth? "Truth is powerful and it prevails."- Sojourner Truth

Word on the Street aka The Wall of Justice

07-2017 T. Dicus "Positive Black People Or Images Are Not Popular To Promote In America, Now That I Know The Truth, I Refuse To Walk In Ignorance. I Will Not Be Ignored. It's Time To Celebrate And Step Into Royalty! We Now Have A Place In History Not Tied To Slavery But Royalty! "

Quote T. Dicus Likes: "The Most Disrespected Person In America Is The Black Woman. The Most Unprotected Person In America Is The Black Woman. The Most Neglected Person In America Is The Black Woman." —May 22, 1962, In Los Angeles, Ca Speech (Https://Mic.Com/Articles/141642/Here-S-The-Malcolm-X-Speech-About-Black-Women-Beyonce-Sampled-In-Lemonade#.Vl4c4ijyf); "Give Your Brain As Much Attention As Your Hair And You'll Be A Thousand Times Better Off." —Malcolm X ; and "True Peace Is Not Merely The Absence Of Tension; It Is The Presence Of Justice." — Dr. Martin Luther King, Jr. Stride Toward Freedom, 1958 And "The Ultimate Measure Of A Man Is Not Where He Stands In Moments Of Convenience And Comfort, But Where He Stands At Times Of Challenge And Controversy." Strength To Love, 1963 — Dr. Martin Luther King, Jr. (See: Https://Www.Nps.Gov/Mlkm/Learn/Quotations.Htm)

07-2017 M Harris. Feels: "In The Past We Were Ignored Unless We Marched. We Want Our History To Be Accepted Just Like The Good And Bad Of Yours." When I Asked Her About The Pledge Of Allegiance Meaning, "Liberty And Justice For All." Her Reply Was "I Must Make The Powers That Be Acknowledge Those Statements To Make Them True For Me".

M. Harris Likes Quote: “If I Didn't Define Myself For Myself, I Would Be Crunched Into Other People's Fantasies For Me And Eaten Alive.” - Audre Lorde

07-2017 Sharon N. Feels: "The Issue Of Whether Queen Calafia Was White Or Black Is A No Issue. There Are No Grey Areas With This, It's Black And White And In Queen Calafia's Case She's Black."

Word on the Street aka The Wall of Justice

Sharon N. Likes Quote: "Your Greatest Regret At The End Of Your Life Will Be The Lions You Didn't Chase. You Will Look Back Longingly On Risks Not Taken, Opportunities Not Seized, And Dreams Not Pursued. Stop Running Away From What Scares You Most And Start Chasing The God-Ordained Opportunities That Cross Your Path." –Mark Batterson

08-2017 Law Professor Dyson, Thomas Jefferson School Of Law Feels: "If You Don't Understand Who You Are, You Don't Know Your Future, And You Won't Know The Full Nature Of Your Enemy."

Professor Dyson Likes Quote: "America Must Get To Work. We Must Dissent From The Indifference; Dissent From A Nation That Buried Its Head In The Sand Waiting In Vain For The Needs Of Its Poor, Its Elderly, And Its Sick To Disappear And Just Blow Away; Dissent From A Government That Has Left Its Young Without Jobs, Education, Or Hope; Dissent From The Poverty Of Vision And The Timeless Absence Of Moral Leadership. We Must Dissent, Because America Can Do Better, Because America Has No Choice But To Do Better." --- Justice Thurgood Marshall Click Here For More Info On Evidence And Actions For Justice Reform: Http://Www.Justicenowforall.Com

09-2017 Lawyer E. Wentworth, Esq. Feels: "Once You Are Aware Of The Truth, You Are Obligated To Make The Change."

09-2017 Law Student S. Thomas Feels: "I Would Be More Proud Of The State Of California If We Have The True Powerful Woman On Our Seal. I Want To Say That I Live In The Land Of Calafía!"

09-2017 Law Student, Native Californian A. Maxwell Feels: "I Was Not Taught The History Of The Name Of California Or That The Black Queen Calafía Of California Is A Black Queen In School At All. It Is Such A Clear Line Of Historical Facts."

Word on the Street aka The Wall of Justice

10-2017 Law Student, Native Californian - T. Adereti Feels: "I Was Taught 'California' Meant Women, Not Black Women. This Is A Significant Difference."

10-2017 Law Student And U.S. Veteran - S. Hunte Feels: "Words Have Meanings. It Is Good To Shine A Light On It. Like The Black Madonna, California Is Similar. You Can't Oppress People Who Believe They Are Strong."

10-2017 Dental Student K. Dicus Feels: "Centuries Of Hiding The Truth Is Ridiculous, It's Too Big To Keep Under The Rug."

10-2017 Retired 88-Year-Old B. Byers Feels: "California Is Black Women? They Want To Keep Us Dumb So We Won't Know Anything."

10-2017 Law Student, Native Californian, T. Davis – Was "Never Taught The Definition Of California. Being Raised By Black Women, [The Definition] Shows The Power Of Black Women...It May Sound Crazy But It Reminds Me Of Wonder Woman®."

11-2017 Tuskegee University Business Executive, J. King - "Black Women Have For Centuries Been The Backbone Of This Nation And Others. We Have Always Been Creators And Educators, The Center And The Circumference. We Have Always Been Queens!We Don't Toot Our Horns All The Time Because We Know And We Know They Know. Learning This History About The Origin Of The Name "California" Was, For This Reason, Not As Much Surprising For Me As It Was Another Confirmation Of Who They Know Us To Be. Our Impact On This World, Both Now And Then, Cannot Be Kept Secret. We Have Been Queens Since The Beginning Of Time. I'm Excited That We Have Decided To Start Recognizing It More, Not Only Internal To Our Community But Externally As Well. It's About Doggone Time!"

Word on the Street aka The Wall of Justice

11-2017 Law Student, Native Californian Says J. Solomon: "This Story Is Wonder Woman®. This Is Systematic Suppression Of Information. If The Government Knew About It, They Don't Want To Empower People Of Color But Would Rather Keep It The Status Quo I.E. Discrimination."

02-2018 Law Professor K.J. Greene, Thomas Jefferson School Of Law - "Words Matter. Symbols Matter. It Is Time To Declare "Times Up" For The Invisible Ways In Which Communities Of Color Have Been Diminished. As Ralph Ellison Said In "Invisible Man": "When I Discover Who I Am, I'll Be Free."

02-2018 Law Professor Semeraro, Thomas Jefferson School Of Law - "Learning History Can Open Our Eyes To The Truth. There's So Much That We Assume That Upon Closer Examination Turns Out To Be False Or Misleading. Ms. Discus's Uncovering Of The Real History Of The California State Seal Is A Breathtaking Example Of How One Person Can Advance Our Understanding Of Our Past And Present And Lead Us Into A More Enlightened Future."

Professor Semeraro Likes - "Some People See Things As They Are And Say Why? I Dream Things That Never Were And Say, Why Not?"- Robert "Bobby" Kennedy

02-21-2018 "Change Only Comes About When Change Agents Care Deeply Enough To Know And Honor Their History." Susan Bisom-Rapp, Associate Dean And Professor Of Law, Thomas Jefferson School Of Law

Note: All law students are of Thomas Jefferson School of Law, except T. Adereti of University of Chicago Law School.

Word on the Street aka The Wall of Justice

2-2018 "Tamra Dicus's Historical Research Is Fascinating And Should Make All Californians (And Americans) Re-Think Our Past." - Professor Wildenthal, Thomas Jefferson School Of Law Professor Wildenthal Likes: "To Travel Hopefully Is A Better Thing Than To Arrive, And The True Success Is To Labor." --Robert Louis Stevenson, 1881

3-2018 T. Byers Of Kansas City: "Jealously Is The Issue. We Must Go Forward, Go Underneath Their Legs, Go Over Their Heads, Or Around His Waist, And Keep It Going. If It Is Of Any Value, It Will Be A Fight."

05-2018 "When You Talk About Black And White...The New Term Is 'Diversity'. Everyone Has A Voice. But You Cannot Loose Your Identity To Diversity." - Lilian Patterson -The Alexandria Black History Museum, Alexandria, Virginia

07-2018 "Tamra Dicus' Work Continues To Challenge The Myth Of White Superiority. The Narrative Of Queen Calafia Has Long Been Hidden In Plain Sight. Dicus Is Having None Of It! "Who Is The Black Queen Calafía Of Golden California?: The Real Wonder Woman" Is A Major Contribution To The Growing Body Of Work That Centers African People's Contributions To World History And Cultures." - Adisa A. Alkebulan, Ph.D., Department Of Africana Studies, San Diego State University

Email the author at queenc@caliisme.com Subject: Wall of Justice for a chance to add your quote to the Wall of Justice or next book regarding Calafía, the first, invisible superhero, Real Wonder Woman, and the Queen of California, namesake of the State of California. Knowledge IS power. Leave a royal legacy.

Math Key (pg. 64):

Superhero	Book	Film	Δ
Queen Calafía	1510	-	-
Superman	1938	1978	40
Wonder Woman	1941	2017	76

SELECTED BIBLIOGRAPHY

Gutiérrez, Diego, 1554-1569, *Americae sive quartae orbis partis nova et exactissima descriptio / avctore Diego Gvtiero Philippi Regis Hisp. etc. Cosmographo ; Hiero. Cock excvde. 1562 ; Hieronymus Cock excude cum gratia et priuilegio* 1562, [Antwerp : s.n.], 1562. Map Link: http://hdl.loc.gov/loc.gmd/g3290.ct000342 (last accessed 1/11/2019).

Garcí Rodríguez de Montalvo (GRM), *Las fergas del muy virtuolo y effozcado cauallero Ef=plandianhijo de Alma=dis de Gaula, Bayerische Staatsbibliothek München*, Germany, pg. 261, 263, URN: bsb10197798, (1526) via Biblioteca de Catalunya, Spain-1526 oldest digitized version.

Garcí Rodríguez de Montalvo (GRM), *El Ramo que de los quatro libros de Amadís sale llamado Las Sergas de Esplandian hijo de Amadís de Gaula, Las quales fueron escriptas por mano dels maestro helisabad porque fuessen magnifiestos los grandes hechos que en armas hizo…*, (Digitized by Google Books) (1510). Link: https://www.caliisme.com/evidence/luzcehl6pzavywwr25xn51i5iqpp7z (last accessed 1/11/19).

Edward E. Hale, *Proceedings of the American Antiquarian Society, The Name of California,* (Worcester, MA), April 30, 45-54 (1862). Courtesy of American Antiquarian Society and Library of Congress.

Edward Everett Hale, *The Queen of California*, The Atlantic Monthly, March, 1864, 265-266. Courtesy of the Harvard University, Schlesinger Library, Boston, Massachusetts.

The Queen of California [From the Atlantic Monthly], Sacramento Daily Union, May 2, 1864, at 6.

George Davidson, *The Origin and the Meaning of the Name California : Calafia the Queen of the Island of California*, (translated "Las Sergas de Esplandaian", San Francisco : Geographical Society of the Pacific), 41, (1910). Courtesy of Library of Congress, Washington, D.C.

Garcí Rodríguez de Montalvo, THE LABORS OF THE VERY BRAVE KNIGHT ESPLANDIÁN (William Thomas Little trans., Center for Medieval and Early Renaissance Studies, State University of New York at Binghamton) (1992). Courtesy of Library of Congress, Washington, D.C.

SELECTED BIBLIOGRAPHY

Papers of William Moulton Marston, 1896-1947, MC 920, (on file with the Schlesinger Library, Harvard University, Boston, Massachusetts).

The Amazon, WMM: Articles Re: Marston and Wonder Woman, 1997, 2001, nd., Schlesinger Library, Harvard University, Boston, Mass.

DC Comics, Wonder Woman source copies at Library of Congress, Washington, D.C., Microfishe © 1992, No. 1, Summer 1942.

Harriet Beecher Stowe, *Sojourner Truth, The Libyan Sibyl*, The Atlantic Monthly 11, no. 66, April 1863, at 473-482. Courtesy of the Library of Congress, Washington, D.C.

J. T. Farnham, esq./Farnham, Thomas Jefferson, The Early Days of California : Embracing What I Saw And Heard There, With Scenes in the Pacific. 1804-1848, 120-121, (Philadelphia, J.E. Potter, 1859). Courtesy of Library of Congress, Washington, D.C.

Editorial, *The Good Name of California Must be Vindicated*, San Francisco Chronicle (1869-Current File); Apr 7, 1877; ProQuest Historical Newspapers: San Francisco Chronicle, at pg. 2.

Arthur L. Price, *How California Got Its Name*, The San Francisco Sunday Call, Nov. 3, 1912, at Section 1.

California: The Golden State, Senate of California, 2010 (https://www.senate.ca.gov/sites/senate.ca.gov/files/the%20golden%20book%202010_0.pdf last accessed 01/16/19). [Color image of Great Seal at pg. 2]

California Government Code § 400 - Design of State Seal

Aya Elamroussi, *Real Meaning of California is #BlackGirlMagic*, The AFRO newspaper, April 19, 2018 (https://www.afro.com/real-meaning-california-blackgirlmagic/ last accessed 01/16/2019).

John Fauvel and Paulus Gerdes, *African Slave and Calculating Prodigy: Bicentenary of the Death of Thomas Fuller,* Academic Press, Historia Mathematica 17 (1990), at 141-151. (https://core.ac.uk/download/pdf/82536820.pdf last accessed 01/16/2019).

SELECTED BIBLIOGRAPHY

Nathan Nunn, Nancy Quin, *The Columbian Exchange: A History of Disease, Food, and Ideas*, Journal of Economic Perspectives, Volume 24, Number 2, (Spring 2010) at pages 163–188. Link: https://www.kellogg.northwestern.edu/faculty/qian/resources/NunnQianJEP.pdf (last accessed 01/19/19).

Bergeron, A. M., Jr. Robert S. Garnett (1819–1861). (2014, June 20). In Encyclopedia Virginia. Retrieved from http://www.EncyclopediaVirginia.org/Garnett_Robert_S_1819-1861 (last accessed 01/19/2019).

María Coduras Bruna, Thesis, LA ANTROPONIMIA EN LOS LIBROS DE CABALLERÍAS ESPAÑOLES: EL CICLO AMADISIANO, 260-261, Universidad de Zaragoza (2013).

Further learning see Professor Henry Gates, Harvard University and PBS: https://mpt.pbslearningmedia.org/collection/africas-great-civilizations/

"If you can control a man's thinking you do not have to worry about his action." — Dr. Carter Godwin Woodson, The Mis-Education of the Negro, Washington, D.C. : Associated Publishers, (1933).

TJSL Law Professor Dyson invited us to NAN in San Diego, my California (2018)

"Whoever controls the images, controls your self-esteem, self-respect and self-development. Whoever controls the history, controls the vision." — Professor Dr. Leonard Jeffries

[T]he **chief witness** in Reconstruction, the **emancipated** slave himself, has been almost **barred** from court. His written Reconstruction record has been largely **destroyed** and nearly always **neglected**. — W.E.B. DuBois, Black Reconstruction in America, pg. 721 (1860-1880). (emphasis added) *From chapter - *The Propaganda of History*

Selected Bibliography

Donate Your Celebrity! Join Us.

Join our movement of lawyers, teachers, quilters, engineers, and future leaders to put a face on the name "California". Until we start to reclaim our name and the truth behind its meaning, no one will see the importance of the Black women Amazon California wonder women meaning. The California historic example of errors show that silence and inaction fuels racism.

Selected Biblography

Real Life *California* Engineers

Brilliant Queen Brittany Blackwell = Queen Calafía

Tuskegee University alumna and an aerospace engineer for the National Aeronautics and Space Administration (NASA) Goddard Space Flight Center.
She also holds a Masters degree, Technical Managment, Johns Hopkins University.

What similarities does she have to Katherine Johnson?

Selected Biblography

Real Life *California* Engineers

Tenacious Ms. Tamra L. Dicus = California Amazon

Tuskegee University alumna chemical engineer, author, and patent examiner at the United States Patent and Trademark Office (USPTO). Fun Fact: I was told that I was the first Black American ever to work on oil rigs in the Gulf of Mexico for Anadrill-Schlumberger. Working in a challenging and demanding field allowed me an opportunity to exude my California courage, intellect, and strength. I also completed two semesters of law school at Thomas Jefferson School of Law. Don't be afraid to stretch your mind. Diversity is needed and valued in STEM. CALIFORNIA IS ME, Queen Calafía is you!

To read more extraordinary examples,
visit www.caliisme.com/california-essence

Selected Biblography

Real Life *California* Lawyers

Magnificent Queen Monique Larmond, Esq. = Queen Calafía

Fun fact: Ms. Larmond was a leader in the first All African-American Women Law Review Managing Board in California (and presumably the nation, while not proven) for Thomas Jefferson School of Law. She was the Managing Editor.

Slay Monique!

Read more here: https://www.tjsl.edu/news-media/2016/15252

Selected Biblography

Real Life *California* Lawyer

Justified Queen Jessica Dance = Queen Calafía

Dr. Martin Luther King, Jr. says, “[I]n your life’s blueprint, there must be a commitment to the eternal principles of beauty, love, and justice...[H]owever young you are, you have a responsibility to seek to make your nation a better nation in which to live. You have a responsibility to seek to make life better for everybody. And so you must be involved in the struggle of freedom and justice.” “The silence of good people is worse than the actions of bad people.” We, the American people, we, the Black community, we Black women, can no longer be silent. "Our time is NOW." - Malalai Joya Jessica dreams of leading the fight for civil rights. She's doing it!

Selected Bibliography

Real *California* Pioneers

The unnamed African ancestors and African descendants of America who initiated the fight for freedom and bore the brunt of enslavement.

We may not have any pictures, but their stories carry on through us from generation to generation.

In the Tuskegee tradition, we must continue "lifting the veil of ignorance" to prove our ancestors did not die in vain and to show gratitude for their suffering. Because our ancestors were prohibited from reading and voting, be encouraged to do what they couldn't.

Note: People continue to ask me, "How did I figure this out?" I will explain in detail in my next book. For now, I submit a few starting points from my experience. I had to:

1. Learn to love my African features enough to value myself to even ask critical questions.
2. Listen to wise elders. For instance, in 2017, my Aunt, Queen Ruth Alexander (R.I.P. 01/30/2019) guided me when I told her of my recent discovery of California's etymology meaning Black women Amazons. She exclaimed, "Uh, Oh! You're shaking up history!" Then, I pulled out my copy of the *Queen of California*, fresh from the Library of Congress to show her. At 91 years old, she could recognize the necessity of what I was merely questionably contemplating over time. Thus, I moved closer to her and I pointed to the column that contained the unrecognizable text, because I didn't recognize the Grecian word. She looked and replied, "You better find out what that means!" So, I did. Eureka! My challenge to the reader: do as our African American ancestors communicated during Slavery, "Each one teach one."

Selected Biblography

Real Life *California* Pioneers

I Sell the Shadow to Support the Substance.
SOJOURNER TRUTH.

REPOSITORY: Library of Congress Prints and Photographs Division Washington, D.C. 20540 USA, DIGITAL ID: (digital file from original item) ppmsca 08979 hdl.loc.gov/loc.pnp/ (digital file from color film copy transparency) cph 3g06166 hdl.loc.gov/loc.pnp/, CARD #: 98501256 Credit Line: Library of Congress, Prints & Photographs Division, [reproduction number, LC-DIG-ppmsca-08979]

Super Queen Sojourner Truth = Queen Calafía

Harriet Beecher Stowe's *Sojourner Truth: The Libyan Sybil* explained just how Truth got her glorious name. That title caught my eye in the summer of 2017 as I scrolled through the microfilm to reach Abolitionist Rev. Hale's *The Queen of California.* Queen Sojourner dictated her fight to reclaim her stolen son. Her mistreatment then may have given her the energy to extemporaneously orate her "Ain't I a Woman?" speech.

Selected Biblography

Real Life *California* Pioneers

Collection of the National Museum of African American History & Culture shared with the Library of Congress.

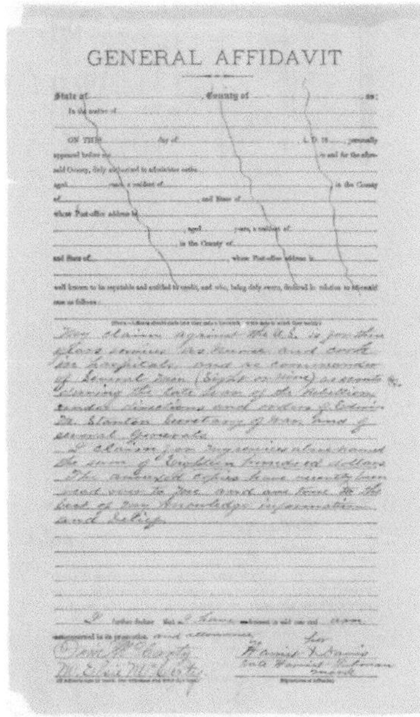

GENERAL AFFIDAVIT

General affidavit of Harriet Tubman relating to her claim for a pension, ca. 1898; Records of the U.S. House of Representatives, National Archives Identifier 306573

Super Heroic Queen Harriet Tubman = Queen Calafía

"My claim against the U.S. is for three years services. As Nurse and cook in hospitals, and as commander of Several Men (Eight or Nine) as scouts during the late war of the Rebellion, under directions and orders of Edwin M. Stanton Secretary of War, and of several Generals. I claim for my services above named the sum of Eighteen hundred dollars. The annexed copies have recently been read over to me and are true to the best of my knowledge information and belief." - Queen Harriet well understood freedom. During the height of Enslavement, self-emancipated Queen Harriet Tubman, left her own husband and family, to help enslaved Black people escape to the North, returning to the Slave territory of the South, sacrificing her own life at least thirteen times. Could you go into such a dangerous place ***13 times***? Persistent, she also filed her complaint. Would you have given up? Tubman helped others become true California Amazons in the fight for freedom! All hail the queen! It is why William Lloyd Garrison gave her the name "Moses". One day, she will be on the $20 bill for her selfless sacrifice for conducting the Underground Railroad so triumphantly during the Civil War. Queen Harriet is the first woman who served in the U.S. military. She was a cook, nurse, and spy for the United States Army. See link: https://www.archives.gov/legislative/resources/education/tubman

Selected Biblography

Do you want to live in the Land of Calafía?
Gather your California courage and continue to fight.
Your voice is a tool; use it at www.caliisme.com.

William Lloyd Garrison

"I am aware that many object to the severity of my language; but is there not cause for severity? I will be as harsh as truth, and as uncompromising as justice. On this subject, I do not wish to think, or to speak, or write, with moderation. No! no! Tell a man whose house is on fire to give a moderate alarm; tell him to moderately rescue his wife from the hands of the ravisher; tell the mother to gradually extricate her babe from the fire into which it has fallen; — but urge me not to use moderation in a cause like the present. I am in earnest — I will not equivocate — I will not excuse — I will not retreat a single inch — AND I WILL BE HEARD."

William Lloyd Garrison, Abolitionist and editor of the Liberator.

Selected Biblography

Your selection of fashion is an outward billboard.
Empower yourself in your wardrobe.

Start the conversation. Stand in **the** truth. Grab CALIFORINA IS ME EST. 1510 bags, dresses, and gear here: Press shop button @ www.caliisme.com

Selected Biblography

Noteworthy Pertinent Quotes

"[I]t is important to show that the oppressed race will not be overlooked; that from this time forward the rights of the neglected race will be recognized to share in all departments of our state government. The Convention will have many things to do to break the spell under which we were laboring. The choice of officers will, therefore, have a political bearing, and cannot be dictated by fitness only. The Convention will meet under very peculiar circumstances — circumstances of originality and grandeur. It will be the first constitutional assembly, the first official body ever convened in the United States without distinction of race or color. It will be the first mixed assemblage, clothed with a public character. As such this Convention has to take a position in immediate contradiction with the old assemblies of the white man's government. They will have to show that a new order will succeed the former order of things, and that the longneglected race will, at last, effectually share in the government of the state.

[T]he chief witness in Reconstruction, the emancipated slave himself, has been almost barred from court. His written Reconstruction record has been largely destroyed and nearly always neglected. Only three or four states have preserved the debates in the Reconstruction conventions; there are few biographies of black leaders. The Negro is refused a hearing because he was poor and ignorant. It is therefore assumed that all Negroes in Reconstruction were ignorant and silly and that therefore a history of Reconstruction in any state can quite ignore him. The result is that most unfair caricatures of Negroes have been carefully preserved; but serious speeches, successful administration and upright character are almost universally ignored and forgotten.

Selected Bibliography

Wherever a black head rises to historic view, it is promptly slain by an adjective—"shrewd", "notorious," "cunning"—or pilloried by a sneer; or put out of view by some quite unproven charge of bad moral character. In other words, every effort has been made to treat the Negro's part in Reconstruction with silence and contempt."

—W.E.B. DuBois, BLACK RECONSTRUCTION IN AMERICA, AN ESSAY TOWARD A HISTORY OF THE PART WHICH BLACK FOLK PLAYED IN THE ATTEMPT TO RECONSTRUCT DEMOCRACY IN AMERICA, 1860-1880, The Propaganda of History, pg. 467, 721 (1935).

"If we are not careful, our colleges will produce a group of close-minded, unscientific, illogical propagandists, consumed with immoral acts. Be careful, 'brethren!' Be careful, teachers!" —Rev. Dr. Martin Luther King, Jr. *The Purpose of Education* from Morehouse College student newspaper, The Maroon Tiger, 1947

Charles Hamilton Houston, graduate of Harvard University, Dean at Howard University Law School, architect of groundbreaking Brown v Topeka, Kansas Board of Education, rejected "separate but equal" schools for African Americans and challenged the U.S. Constitution. Houston said, "A lawyer's either a social engineer or . . . a parasite on society . . . ." Smithsonian American History Museum, Washington, D.C., Separate Is Not Equal, Link: http://americanhistory.si.edu/brown/history/3-organized/charles-houston.html.

If I have been inspired by Her Majesty Queen Calafía and her California Black women Amazons, just think of what you can dream, imagine, create and innovate. I was so shaken with inspiration that I invented that "Solve This!" formula. I took it to a STEM high school class in N.E., Washingotn D.C. One girl was so moved when I asked them how it felt to know a Black woman's name and likeness is in the name California. She broke her silence of two years and repeated, "They don't do nothin' for Black girls." Together, yes, we can do something for all Calafías. We can speak the truth. We can fight for truth. California Royalty, write your dreams down below, study, pursue them, and surround yourself knowledge daily.

1. Hint, hint: #RevealTheSeal____________

2. ____

3. ____

Booker T. Washington, founder of Tuskegee University, said, "[S]uccess is to be measured not so much by the position that one has reached in life as by the obstacles which he has overcome while trying to succeed." Booker T. Washington, UP FROM SLAVERY: AN AUTOBIOGRAPHY, 39 (1901).

Selected Bibliography

Black Women contributed majestically
and birthed America's rich making. Our
souls carry an invisible badge of honor.
The California crown is rightfully ours.

"Our crown
has been bought
and
paid for.
All
we have to do
is wear it."
— James Baldwin

Yet, we know, "Power concedes
nothing without a demand."
— Fredrick Douglass

No, her first name *ain't* Minerva or Diana. It's Calafía.
Queen Calafía—ruler of golden-black California. #RealFacts
Educate. Celebrate. Act! Thanks, Ms. Jackson.

QUESTION PRESENTED

Do you think that there is, officially, an accurate
portrayal of Queen Calafía in the California Great
Seal anywhere in the United States of America?
Seek and ye shall find.

Selected Biblography

It is uniquely significant that the very first documented sentence of the very first name of a state in the United States of America was the *Spanish* Renaissance invented name *California*; and that Black Women (*mujeres negras*) only, Amazons (*Amazonas*), and gold (*oro*) occupies its comic etymology. Dually, the invented *California* name highlights accurate, real history and also comic book history. Examine the given California quotations A-D:

1510 NOVEL QUOTATION A

In Spanish, "California" means this-
Sabed que a la diestra mano de las Indias existe una isla llamada California muy cerca de un costado del Paraíso Terrenal; y estaba poblada por mujeres negras, sin que existiera allí un hombre, pues vivían a la manera de las amazonas. Eran de bellos y robustos cuerpos, fogoso valor y gran fuerza. Su isla era la más fuerte de todo el mundo, con sus escarpados farallones y sus pétreas costas. Sus armas eran todas de oro y del mismo metal eran los arneses de las bestias salvajes que ellas acostumbraban domar para montarlas, porque en toda la isla no había otro metal que el oro.

Source: Gutenberg and Google Books, Rodríguez de Montalvo, *Sergas*, (1510)

1864 QUOTATION B

"Know that, on the right hand of the Indies, there is an island called California, very near to the Terrestrial Paradise, which was peopled with black women, without any men among them, because they were accustomed to live after the fashion of Amazons. They were of strong and hardened bodies, of ardent courage, and of great force. The island was the strongest in the world, from its steep rocks and great cliffs. Their arms were all of gold; and so were the caparisons of the wild beasts which they rode, after having tamed them; for in all the island there is no other metal."

Source: Rev. Mr. Edward Everett Hale, *Queen of California*, The Atlantic Monthly, March, (1864), at Page 267 (footnote omitted on Columbus, emphasis intentional).

Selected Bibliography

2010 QUOTATION C

In English, "California" is edited to mean this-

"'Know then, that **west** of the Indies, but to the east of Eden, lies California, an island peopled by **a swarthy**, robust, passionate race of women living **manless** like Amazons. Their island, the most rugged in the world, abounds in gold. Having no other metal, all their arms and armor are made of this gold.'" "The powerful Queen Calafía was said to rule over this fabulous country."

Source: By California Senate pamphlet "*California Golden State*", (2010), at page 1. Referencing Edward Everett Hale earlier but source is omitted. (emphasis intentional).

2017 QUOTATION D

In English, "California" meaning is this -

"It is known that to the right of the Indies there exists an island called California very near the terrestrial paradise; and peopled by Black women among whom there was not a single man since they lived in the way of the Amazons. They had beautiful robust bodies, spirited courage and great strength."

Source: By The AFRO Newspaper via Project Gutenberg http://central.gutenberg.org/articles/eng/Origin_of_the_name_California (last accessed 04/19/2018) via Encyclopedia, W. H. (2017). World Heritage Encyclopedia. Retrieved from http://www.self.gutenberg.org/

QUESTION: Which are the correct quotations? What words were altered? What words were omitted?

ACT: Slay the wrong quotation, circle the right quotations and do something about it if you feel what have read above disturbs you. Is this grammatically correct? Is this ethically correct? How do you feel when someone does not accept you and attempts to change your identity?

Act! Goal: Awareness. Feel free to tear this page out. Circulate and Distribute. Visit caliisme.com/media

- DID YOU KNOW THE STATE SEAL OF CALIFORNIA WAS DESIGNED BY A CONFEDERATE VIRGINIA GENERAL WHO MURDERED CHIEF TUSKEGEE'S SEMINOLE INDIANS & BLACKS IN THE SEMINOLE WAR AND MEXICANS IN THE MEXICAN AMERICAN WAR?

- DID YOU KNOW WONDER WOMAN® IS REALLY THE BLACK QUEEN CALAFÍA AND ROMAN MINERVA IS REALLY SUPPOSED TO BE THE EGYPTIAN GODDESS NÊITH OR QUEEN CALAFÍA IN THE GREAT SEAL OF CALIFORNIA? BOTH SHOULD BE ANCIENT BLACK WOMEN IMAGES.

- DID YOU KNOW CALIFORNIA REALLY MEANS A GOLDEN ISLAND OF STRONG, BEAUTIFUL, COURAGEOUS, & HARD-WORKING BLACK WOMEN RULED BY QUEEN CALAFÍA FROM AN ANCIENT SPANISH NOVEL? THE STATE SEAL SHOULD REALLY BE:

HISTORICALLY INACCURATE – Est. 1849

HISTORICALLY ACCURATE – Est. 1510

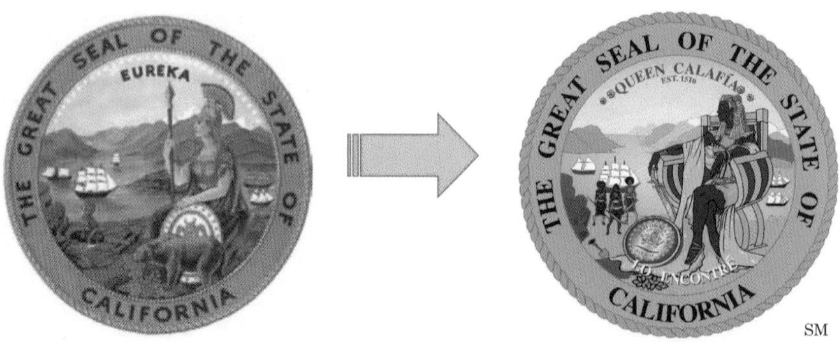

SOURCE: SENATE OF CALIFORNIA

SOURCE: CALIFORNIA IS ME

"Knowledge will forever govern ignorance: And a people who mean to be their own Governors, must arm themselves with the power which knowledge gives." — James Madison (1822) Link: https://www.loc.gov/resource/mjm.20_0155_0159/?sp=1&st=text

Printed in Great Britain
by Amazon

87417627R00060